بسم الله الرحمن الرحيم

# 10 AMAZING SHEIKHAHS

# 10 AMAZING SHEIKHAHS

*by*

GADIJA BESTER

ALIF ACADEMY
FOR QURANIC SCIENCES

al-Tanzil
INSTITUTE OF QURANIC SCIENCES

**Alif Academy for Quranic Sciences**
Cape Town, South Africa
(+27) 74 665 0786
alifacademyconnect@gmail.com

**al-Tanzil Institute of Quranic Sciences**
Cape Town, South Africa
+27 72 141 7977
info@al-tanzil.co.za

**HA-MEEM PUBLICATIONS**
www.hameemstore.com
@hameemstore
orders@hameemstore.com
+1 (416) 879-2545

**First Authorized Edition 2024**

# Alif Academy
# For Quranic Sciences

Alif Academy for Quranic Sciences
11 Farmfield Road, Schaapkraal,
Cape Town, 7941, South Africa

Tel: (+27) 74 665 0786
E-mail: alifacademyconnect@gmail.com

**Subject: Grant of Permission to Publish and Copyrights for All Works**

Dear HA-MEEM Publications,

Assalāmu ʾAlaykum wa RaḥmatuLlahi wa Barakātuhū,

I am writing to formally grant Ha-Meem Publications permission to publish, distribute, and manage the copyrights of all my works, including books, articles, and other authored materials. This consent covers all formats, both print and digital.

Please consider this letter as my official authorization for the management and publication of these works, with the expectation that the integrity of the content will be maintained.

JazākumuLlāhu Khayran for your co-operation.

Sincerely,
Gadija Bester

وَأَسْأَلُهُ عَـوْنِي عَـلَىٰ مَا نَـوَيْـتُهُ
وَحِفْظِيَ فِي دِيْنِيْ إِلَىٰ مُنْتَهَىٰ عُمْرِي

وَأَسْأَلُهُ عَنِّي التَّجَاوُزَ فِي غَدٍ
فَمَا زَالَ ذَا عَفْوٍ جَمِيْلٍ وَذَا غَفْرِ

*I ask Him to assist me upon what I have intended, and (I ask Allah for) protection in my religion until the end of my life.*

*And I ask Him to forgive me tomorrow, for He remains the possessor of good pardon and the possessor of forgiveness.*

# Table of Contents

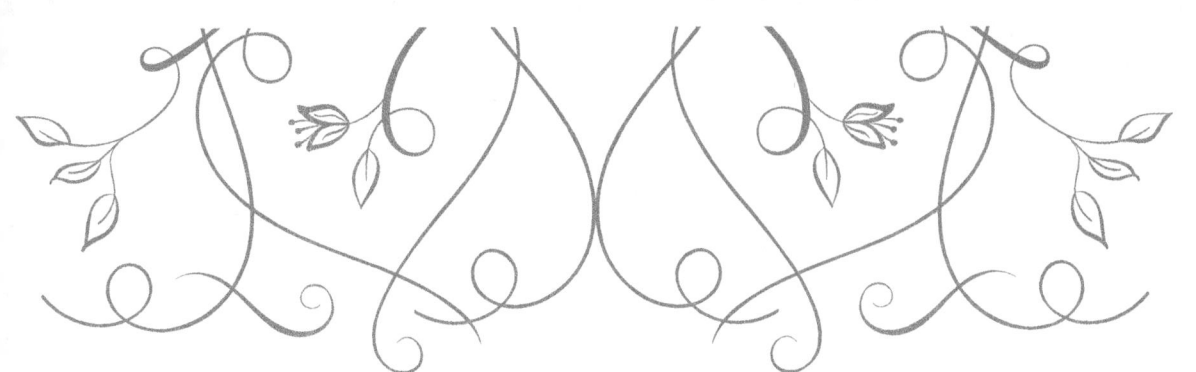

# *Acknowledgements*

First and foremost, all praises and gratitude are to Allah, the Almighty, for allowing me to complete this publication and share the stories of these illustrious Sheikhahs with everyone.

I cannot express enough gratitude to my teacher, Mawlana Salīm Gaibie, for his continued support and encouragement, without which the completion of this publication might not have been accomplished.

A huge appreciation goes to TAKA for their generous support and contribution in making the publication of this book possible.

Additionally, I'd like to express my deepest gratitude to all those involved in the editing process of this book, especially Malika from Quality Quill Editing, Nielfa from Folio Works, and my colleague, Naadirah Khan, for her valued support and for reading through the translation and biographies in its initial stages.

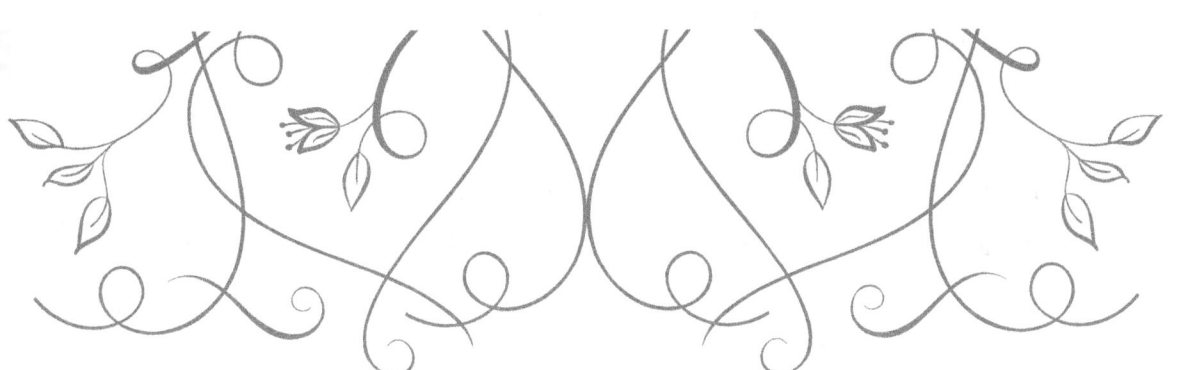

Finally, I would like to acknowledge with gratitude the support and love of my beloved parents, Rowaydah and Moghamat Shahien Bester, as well as my Muʿallimah, Ayeshah Siddeeqah Slarmie, my colleagues at DUAI INĀTH, and my peers at al-Tanzīl Institute for always inspiring and motivating me.

# Foreword

*In the Name of Allah, Most Gracious, Most Merciful*

It is with immeasurable pride that I read the work of our esteemed Muʿallimah Gadija Bester. Her work highlights the profound reverence accorded to the bearers and teachers of the Noble Qurʾān and is a celebration of the legacy and divine preservation of the Qurʾān through the annals of Islamic history.

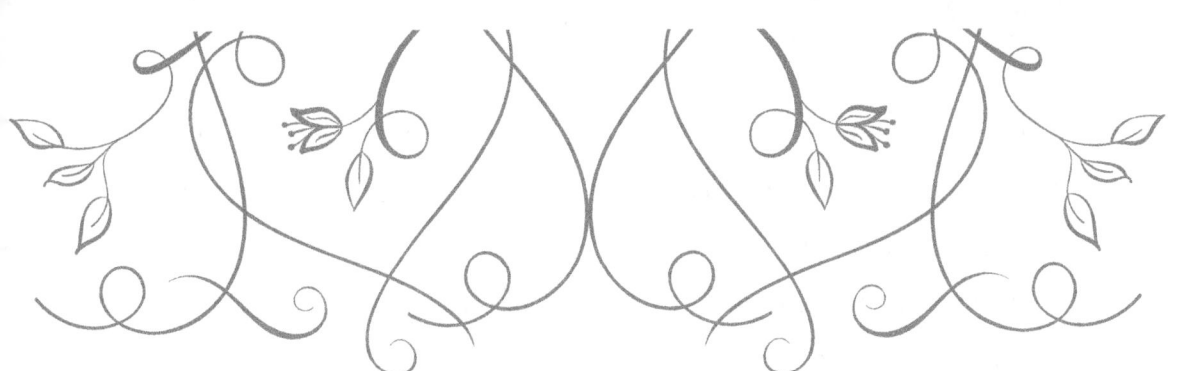

This divine preservation is the design of our Supreme Bestower ﷻ, facilitated by the love and dedication of many great men and women who have come before us. This literary work illustrates the contribution of many female luminaries in the learning and propagation of the Divine Word. Islam has never shied away from female scholarship; rather, it has always been part of the fabric of our dīn. We need not look further than the teacher of teachers, our mother Aishah رضي الله عنها. Reflecting on her life and the lives of so many others, notably those luminaries mentioned in this work, humbles us as a Muslim community and reminds us of the collective responsibility we are charged with. For Islam to continue to prosper, scholarship must continue to prosper too, with opportunities freely available to both males and females.

This work also highlights the bedrock of our entire faith and the pride of every Muslim: the reality that our entire dīn, more specifically the transmission of the Qurʾān, is based on *isnad* i.e. transmission chains linking every reciter to their teachers and those before them until the chain eventually ends at our beloved Prophet ﷺ.

Documenting the life stories and accomplishments of our Qurʾānic scholars is essential. It is vital that we preserve the legacy of the Qurʾān and exceptional scholarship for all future generations, just as it is vital that future generations have a model of scholarship to emulate. This literary contribution highlights the growth we have reached as a community. In the early 1990s, very few females were memorising the Qurʾān full-time in Cape Town. Today, following the efforts of Muʿallimah Gadija, her teachers, and countless other females in the Cape, we are witnessing a revival of female scholarship in the area of Qurʾān.

I commend Muʿallimah Gadija on this momentous work, pray that Allah ﷻ accepts it, and trust that it inspires all who read it.

**MUʾALLIMAH RUKAYYA SAMSODIEN**

Director and Lecturer at Baseerah Institute

# *Introduction*

This booklet presents a glimpse into the lives of 10 extraordinary females who dedicated their lives to the service of the Qur'ān, studying it and imparting its knowledge to others. People – male and female – from all over the world travelled to them to benefit from their Qur'ānic insight and expertise.

I have collected the biographical information of these Sheikhahs from the writings of my teacher, Mawlana Salīm Gaibie, various books and articles – in print and on social media – as well as via interviews. I hope to highlight the role these Sheikhahs played in preserving the legacy of the Qur'ān. Particularly important in their biographies are the names of their teachers from whom they have grasped their knowledge and their students to whom they have imparted their knowledge. To demonstrate this, a selection of noteworthy teachers and students have been listed after each Sheikhah's biography. In this way, just like these amazing Sheikhahs, the names of their teachers and students will forever be etched into the history of Qur'ānic scholarship.

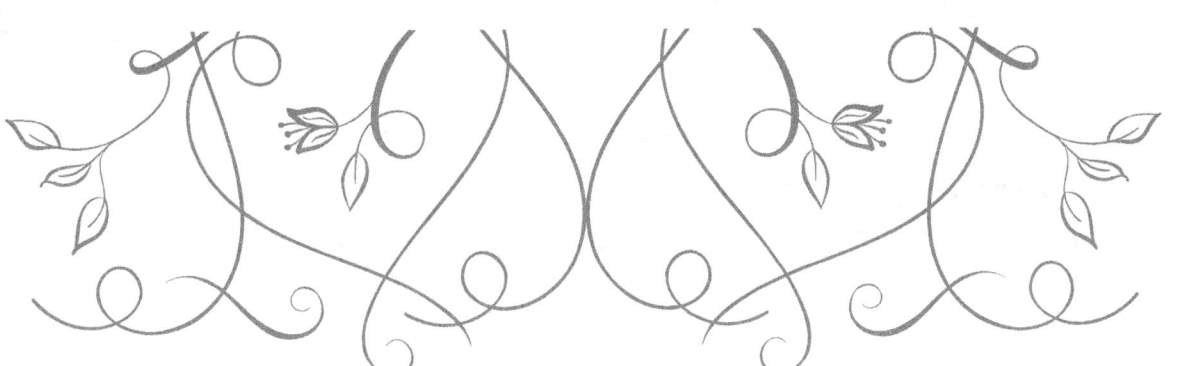

The biographies are in no particular order of appearance. However, I start with a Sheikhah from Cape Town – regarded as being the first female *ḥāfiṭḥah* in the Cape – and again end with a Capetonian, the first female in South Africa to have studied and received *ijāzah* in the 14 *Qirā'āt*; the Major 10 *Qirā'āt* as well as the Four *Shādhdh Qirā'āt* (extra-canonical Qur'ānic Readings).

The penultimate biography is of Sheikhah Amat-Allah. Although she was a *ḥāfiṭḥah* of the Qur'ān, she chose to dedicate her life to the science of hadith, which illustrates the diversity of female scholarship.

At the end of each biography, I mention my *sanad* (chain of transmission) to these amazing Sheikhahs; firstly, how I transmit texts from these Sheikhahs, and secondly, how I transmit the *Qirā'āt* (Qur'ānic Readings) from them. In some cases, I only transmit texts from these Sheikhahs. In the case of Sheikhah Amat-Allah, I transmit *ḥadīth*, amongst other sciences. The objective behind mentioning the *asānīd* (chains of transmission) is to show that in addition to the historical value, abilities, and scholarship of these females, a student is able to forge a link between themselves and these Sheikhas, making them a part of their scholarly lineage. While these Sheikhas have passed on, their legacies are eternal. Likewise, a student will eventually die, but their legacies may remain forever.

Through the lives of these women and the many other brilliant female scholars, we should be aware that men and women shared equal responsibilities in the acquisition and propagation of knowledge, albeit within the confines of Islam.

While previously females might have found it difficult or challenging to study because they had to travel, at times to other countries, recently, many institutions dedicated to female learning and scholarship have been established locally. With the onset of Covid-19, online studying has become very common, making it even easier for females to acquire knowledge. May Allah allow us to seek out these opportunities and allow us to take maximum benefit from our scholars.

I hope that the biographies of these exceptional Sheikhahs encourage and inspire its readers to study the Qurʾān and become a part of the legacy of preserving it, whether with regards to its reading, memorisation, translation, or interpretation.

May Allah enrich our lives with the beauty and grandeur of the Qurʾān. May He accept the little effort we make for His Book and grant us *tawfīq* (divine ability) to do more to serve Him. May we strive to make the Qurʾān our companion so that it may intercede for us on the day of *Qiyāmah* and accompany us in our graves. *Āmīn.*

**GADIJA BESTER**

# *My Asānīd – chains of transmission – to these Sheikhahs*

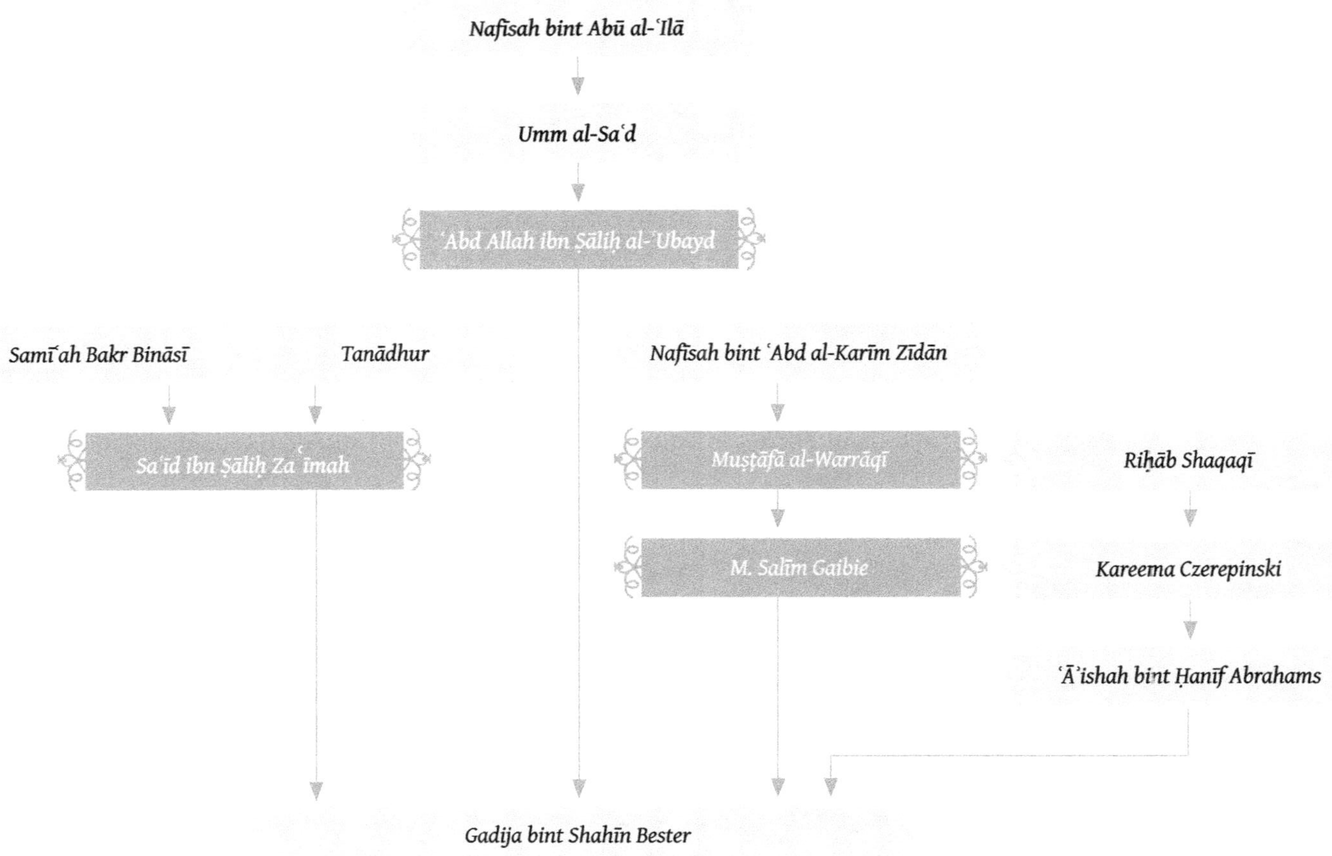

# The Asānīd of these Sheikhahs to ʿAlī al-Badrī

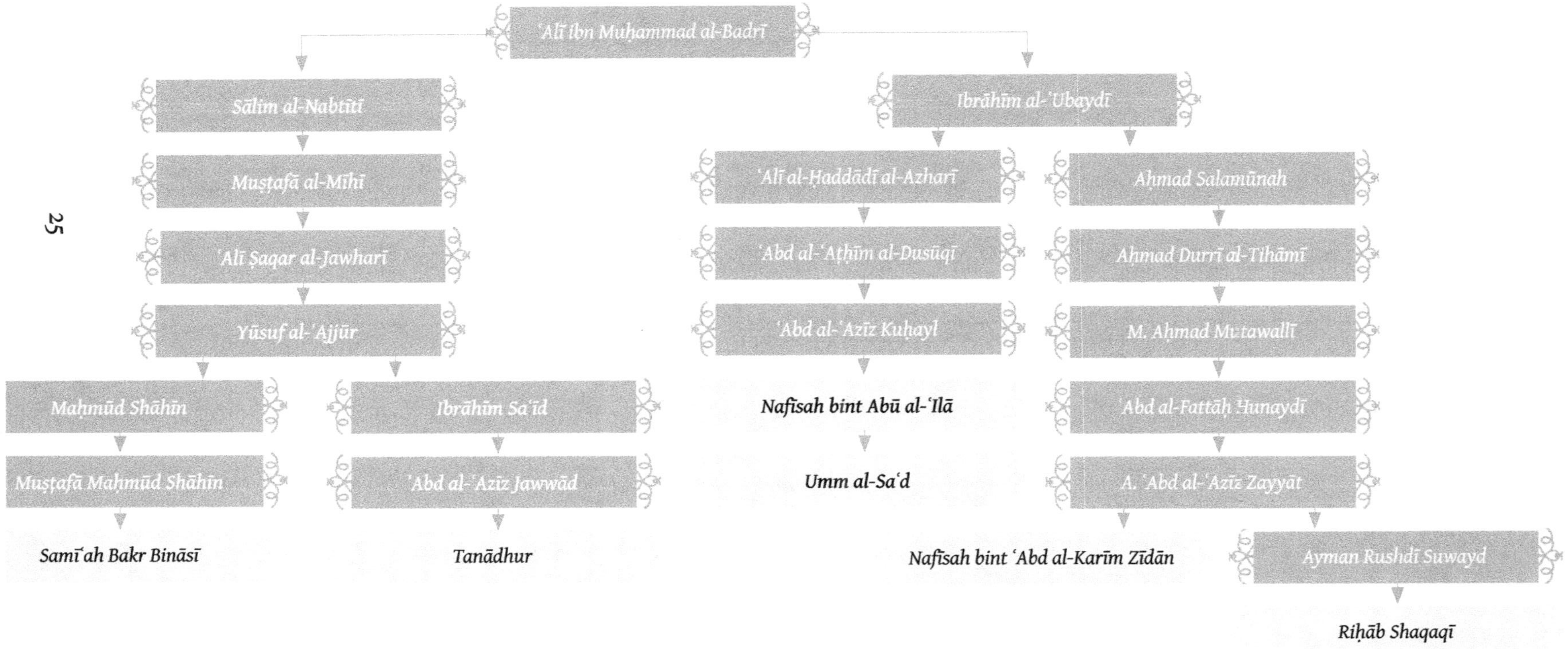

## *The Sanad of Sheikh ʿAlī al-Badrī to the Prophet* ﷺ

Prophet Muḥammad ﷺ

*ʿAlī ibn Abī Ṭālib* رضي الله عنه *(d. 40)*

*Abū ʿAbd al-Raḥmān Sulamī (d. 74)*

*ʿĀṣim ibn Abī al-Najūd (d. 127)*

*Ḥafṣ ibn Sulaymān (d. 180)*

*ʿUbayd ibn al-Ṣabbāḥ (d. 235)*

*Abū al-ʿAbbās al-Ushnānī (d. 307)*

*Abū al-Ḥasan al-Hāshimī (d. 368)*

*Ṭāhir ibn Ghalbūn (d. 399)*

*Abū ʿAmr al-Dānī (d. 444)*

*Abū Dāwūd Ibn Najāḥ (d. 496)*

*ʿAlī ibn Hudhayl al-Balansī (d. 564)*

*Imam al-Shāṭibī (d. 590)*

*Kamāl ʿAlī ibn Shujāʿ (d. 661)*

*Taqiyy al-Dīn al-Ṣāʾigh (d. 725)*

*Ibn al-Baghdādī (d. 781)*

*Muḥammad ibn al-Jazarī (d. 833)*

*Riḍwān al-ʿUqbī (d. 852)*

*Zakariyyā al-Anṣārī (d. 926)*

*Nāṣir al-Dīn al-Ṭablāwī (d. 966)*

*Shiḥādhah al-Yamanī (d. 987)*

*Muḥammad al-Baqarī (d. 1111)*

*Aḥmad al-Baqarī (d. 1189)*

*ʿAlī ibn Muḥammad al-Badrī (d. 1199)*

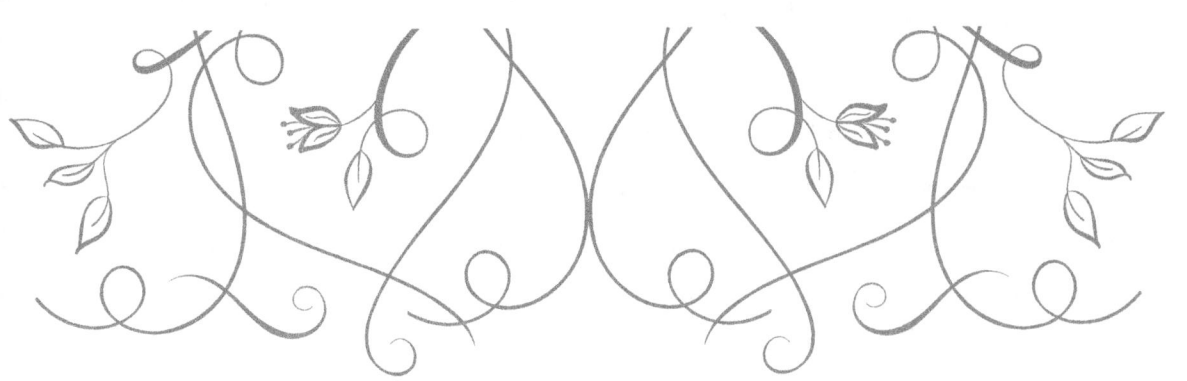

# 1

## *Ḥāfiṭḥah Fāṭimah Geyer*

1906-1994

The story of Fāṭimah Geyer, who was fondly known as 'Ma Geyer', is an inspiring one.[1] What is unique about her story is that she is documented as being one of the first female memorisers of the Qur'ān (*ḥāfiṭḥāt*) in Cape Town. Her siblings called her 'Ma' – which means 'mother' in Afrikaans – when their mother had passed away, and she had subsequently assumed the responsibility of raising them. Thereafter, her own children started calling her 'Ma', and she fondly became known to most as 'Ma Geyer'.

1. The information was predominantly gathered via an interview with Ma Geyer's daughters, Zuleiga Amlay and Mariam Wadvalla. Though her name is spelt as 'Geyer', it is pronounced as 'Khayr', which means goodness and excellence in Arabic.

She was an attentive, independent, God-fearing, witty, dependable, and wise lady. She was fully aware and alert until the day she passed away. Ma Geyer could not read nor write but had memorised the Qur'ān extremely well. Despite spending most of her life caring for and raising her siblings, children, and grandchildren, she never neglected her relationship with the Qur'ān.

Fāṭimah Geyer was born in Bo-Kaap in April 1906, daughter to Imam ʿAbd al-Malik Ḥamzah.[2] She was also the great-granddaughter of Imam Achmat van Bengalen (1750-1843) and Saartjie (Sarah) van de Kaap (1775-1847). Saartjie van de Kaap is well-known in Cape Muslim history for having bequeathed her land for the building of the first mosque in South Africa, the Awwal Masjid in Dorp Street, Bo-Kaap.

As was customary during that period, Fāṭimah was sent to school when she reached the age of six. She had an astounding memory. After hearing a hymn at school, she easily committed it to memory. Her father, Imam ʿAbd al-Malik, heard her singing this hymn she had learned at school. Amazed that she had so easily memorised the hymn, he encouraged her to start memorising the Qur'ān instead. At that point, her father kept her home, and she never returned to school.

Fāṭimah began memorising the Qur'ān at the age of six. She completed her *ḥifṭḥ* (memorisation) within two years. Imam ʿAbd al-Malik had great plans for his daughter; she was meant to learn Arabic and further her studies just like her father did in Mecca. However, Fāṭimah's mother

2. He was ʿAbd al-Malik Ḥamzah. As a small child, he accompanied his parents for hajj and then remained in Mecca for a period of about 20 years. He benefitted and studied under the choicest *mashāyikh* (teachers) and spiritual guides of Mecca during that time. Some of his teachers included the famous *muqri'* (teacher of *Qirā'āt*), Sheikh Muḥammad al-Sharbīnī al-Dimyāṭī (d. 1321/1903), and the famous *muḥaddith* (hadith transmitter), Sheikh Ḥasan Mash-shāṭ (d. 1399/1979).

passed away when she was only 10 years old. From that tender age, she took care of her siblings and assisted her father in raising them.[3]

At the age of 25, she got married and had eight of her own children; four boys and four girls. Many people requested Ma Geyer to teach their children, but she felt like she would not do them justice due to having the responsibility of raising her eight children, as well as caring for her siblings. As busy as Ma Geyer was, she never abandoned or neglected the Qurʾān. At the age of 35, she was widowed, with her youngest daughter being only three months old at the time.

When Ma Geyer's husband passed away, her father, Imam ʿAbd al-Malik, was living in Johannesburg. Being widowed with eight children and no income, her father wanted her to come to Johannesburg with her children and stay with him. She declined the offer and told her father that she still needed to take care of her father-in-law and that he should not worry about her. She assured him that the Qurʾān would look after her in the same manner that she had been looking after the Qurʾān through all the years.

It was Fāṭimah's habit to prepare the household's lunches in the morning before they left for work or school. Her preparation followed a particular procedure of first laying out the slices of bread and then preparing them each individually. This took much time to prepare, and occasionally the household would get impatient because they needed to

---

3. Ma Geyer and three of her brothers learned under the tutelage of their father. Her brothers were Imam Ṭāhir, ʿAbd al-Ḥamīd, and Ḥamzah. Her eldest brother, Imam Ṭāhir Malik, was the first local to complete the recitation of the entire Qurʾān in just two units of Prayer (two *rakaʿāt*). This extraordinary feat is part of Cape Town's oral history, oft-repeated amongst reciters and teachers of the Qurʾān. Professor Da Costa records that the entire Qurʾān was recited in four units of Prayer, not two, and that it lasted from after the *Tarāwīḥ* Prayer until the *Fajr* Prayer. See *Pages from Cape Muslim History*: 160.

leave. Her response to their impatience was that on every slice of bread, she recited a portion of the Qurʾān and prayed for the person she was preparing it for.

In an interview with her two daughters, her daughter Zuleiga mentioned that whenever their mother prepared their meals, she would take her time and recite on every slice of bread while making *duʿā* that Allah protects them.

In 1965, Ma Geyer travelled to Mecca for hajj. At almost every port she stopped, people enquired about her—the *ḥāfiṭḥah* who was on the boat. When she stopped at Cairo on her return home from hajj, the famous Sheikh ʿAbd al-Bāsiṭ ʿAbd al-Ṣamad heard about her and invited her for a meal. She accepted the invitation and took along all the pilgrims who were with her. When they were done eating, Sheikh ʿAbd al-Bāsiṭ read something from the Qurʾān and tested her memorisation. In this manner, Fāṭimah was examined by the esteemed Sheikh ʿAbd al-Bāsiṭ and had the privilege of reciting to him. This was an incredibly memorable visit for her.

Though she was considered illiterate because she had no formal schooling, she had memorised the Qurʾān, understood the meanings of what she was reciting, and was able to write the Qurʾān as well as in Arabic. She would often write verses of the Qurʾān on paper and place them around the house for blessings and protection. She lamented that younger students of the Qurʾān did not understand what they were reciting and did not appreciate its meanings. She revised the Qur'ān in the early hours of the morning and habitually recited it at night. Though she never recited in public, she had a melodious voice, and when she recited at night in her room, the entire household would be mesmerised by her beautiful recitation. One of her favourite *sūrahs* was Sūrat al-Raḥmān.

Allah gifted Ḥajjah Fāṭimah with the opportunity to learn the Qur'ān. It was her most prized possession. Her life was built on faith, dependence on Allah, and an intense love for the Qur'ān. The Qur'ān looked after her just as she looked after it. She believed that it protected her, sustained her; that it kept her mind fresh and alert. She *lived* the Qur'ān and advised others with the Qur'ān. Many of the local *ḥuffāṭh*, like Sheikh Ṣāliḥ 'Abādī and Sheikh Yūsuf Gabier, revered her for her memorisation of the Qur'ān. Even after her demise, Sheikh Ṣāliḥ 'Abādī showed great reverence to her children for the sole fact that they were the progeny of a great *ḥāfiṭhah* of the Qur'ān. Whatever explanations and meanings she had learned about the Qur'ān from her father, she imparted to others whenever she was afforded the opportunity to do so.

**Teachers:**

- Her father, Imam 'Abd al-Malik Ḥamzah, under whom she memorised the Qur'ān, learned Arabic, and grasped the understanding of the Qur'ān.

**Students:**

- She had no formal students. However, Sheikh Yūsuf Gabier revised the Qur'ān with her. She would also occasionally ask Sheikh Hāshim Julies to recite to her.

The feat of Imam Ṭāhir reciting the entire Qurʾān took six hours and occurred in Durban in the month of Ramaḍān, 1346/1927, according to this plaque.

On her last, Sheikh Ṣāliḥ ʿAbādī and his students were amongst those who were reciting by her. Ma Geyer passed away in the year 1994 at the age of 88.

*A plaque presented as testimony to Ḥāfiṭh Ṭāhir reciting the entire Qurʾān in two units*

## My Link

I am not linked to Ma Geyer. However, I am linked to her father, Imam ʿAbd al-Malik, by way of sharing a link to his teachers: the Qurʾānic expert, Sheikh Muḥammad Sharbīnī, and the hadith expert, Sheikh Ḥasan Mash-shāṭ.

I received *ijāzah* from my teacher, the *muqriʾ*, Sheikh ***ʿAbd Allah ibn Ṣāliḥ ibn Muḥammad al-ʿUbayd,*** who received *ijāzah* from Sheikh ***ʿAbd al-Qādir ibn Karāmat-Allah al-Bukhārī,*** who received *ijāzah* from Sheikh ***Muḥammad ʿAbd al-Bāqī al-Lucknawī,*** who received *ijāzah* from Sheikh ***Muḥammad Sharbīnī.***

I received *ijāzah* from our teacher in Cape Town, the polymath, Mufti ***Muḥammad Ṭāhā Karaan,*** who received *ijāzah* from the erudite *muḥaddith*, Sheikh ***Muḥammad ʿAwwāmah,*** who received *ijāzah* from Sheikh ***Ḥasan Mash-shāṭ.***

# 2

## *Sheikhah Umm al-Saʿd*

1925-2006

Sheikhah Umm al-Saʿd[4] bint Muḥammad ibn ʿAlī ibn Najm was born in 1343/1925 in Manūfiyyah, Egypt. She lost her eyesight at the age of two. Due to her father's work, they moved and settled in Alexandria.

She started her memorisation of the Qurʾān at the age of five and completed it when she was ten years old. At the age of 15, she went to Sheikhah Nafīsah bint Abū al-ʿIlā to study *Qirāʾāt*. Sheikhah Nafīsah dedicated her life to the teaching of the Qurʾān and *Qirāʾāt*. Despite the many marriage proposals she received, she never married and chose to teach the Qurʾān instead. She also became very despondent in that many of her female students, upon whom she had sacrificed much time and effort, neglected to teach what they had gained from her after getting married. Thus, when Sheikhah Umm al-Saʿd came to her, she agreed to teach her *Qirāʾāt* on the very unusual condition that she would not get married. Sheikhah Umm al-Saʿd agreed to this condition. It was in this manner that she read the 10 *Qirāʾāt* via the *Shāṭibiyyah* and the *Durrah* to

4. *Imtāʿ al-Fuḍalāʾ bi Tarājim al-Qurrāʾ*: 5/95.

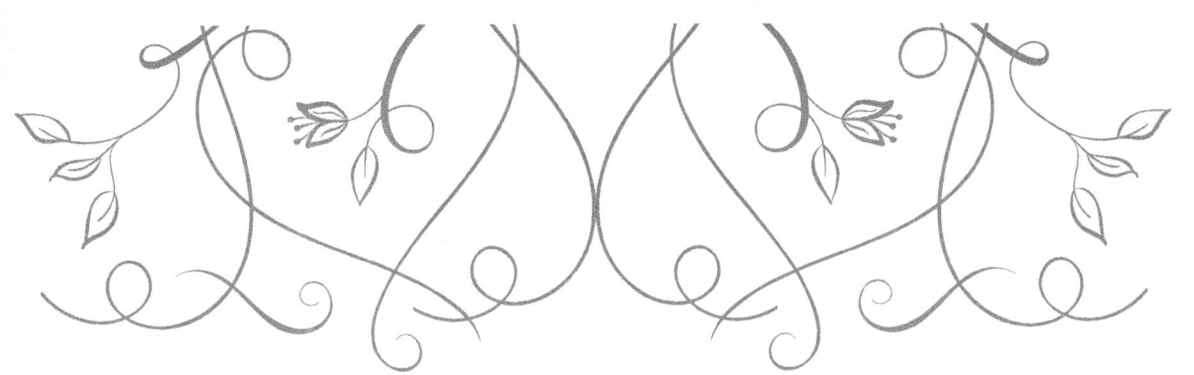

Sheikhah Nafīsah. At the age of 23, she completed her study of the 10 *Qirāʾāt*.

Thereafter, she started teaching *Qirāʾāt* in Alexandria. Because she was blind, not much occupied her except the Qurʾān and *Qirāʾāt*. Her mind was thoroughly engrossed with none other than the Qurʾān and the texts of *Tajwīd* and *Qirāʾāt* that she had memorised. It was, therefore, not unsurprising that she became an expert in these sciences. All over the world, the name of Umm al-Saʿd was known, not only for her expertise and proficiency in the science of *Qirāʾāt* but also for her high *sanad* (chain of transmission). Men and women from all around the world travelled to read *Qirāʾāt* to her. She would teach women from 8 am until 2 pm, and the men from 2 pm until 8 pm in the evening. They would only break for prayers, eating, and other necessary duties. In 1999, she spent 10 months in Riyadh, where many read and benefitted from her. For 60 years, she continued teaching the Qurʾān in this manner. Towards the end of her life, she stated: "60 years of memorising and revising the Qurʾān and its *Qirāʾāt* has made it such that I cannot forget anything of it. I know every verse of the Qurʾān, in which *sūrah* it appears, which *juz* it is in, its *mutashābihāt* (similar verses), and how to read it in all its different *Qirāʾāt*. It is as if I know the Qurʾān like my very name. I do not sense that I would forget or falter in it because there is nothing else I know except the Qurʾān and *Qirāʾāt*."

The happiest days in the Sheikhah's life were whenever a *khatm* of the Qurʾān was made, whether it was in only one narration, in one *Qirāʾāh*, or all 10 *Qirāʾāt*. On such days, everyone came together and joined in the meals prepared for this joyous occasion.

After the demise of her teacher, she received a marriage proposal from one of her students who had completed the 10 *Qirāʾāt* by her: Sheikh

Muḥammad Farīd Nuʿmān. Like her, he was also blind and had dedicated his life to the Qurʾān. Though they remained married for 40 years, they had no children. However, between them, they had countless students. When she was asked concerning her students, she replied that she could recall every single one of them, including what they had read to her.

**Teachers:**

- Nafīsah bint Abū al-ʿIlā, to whom she read the 10 *Qirāʾāt* via the *Shāṭibiyyah* and the *Durrah.*

**Students:**

- Her husband, Sheikh Muḥammad Farīd Nuʿmān.
- The famous reciter, Sheikh Aḥmad Naʿīnaʿ.
- My teacher, Sheikh ʿAbd Allah ibn Ṣāliḥ al-ʿUbayd.

She died on 17 Ramaḍān 1427/9 October 2006.

*Sheikhah Umm al-Saʿd receiving an award for her service rendered to the Qurʾān*

### My Link to Sheikhah Umm al-Saʿd

***In Qurʾān:*** I read the Seven *Qirāʾāt* via the *Shāṭibiyyah* to my Muʿallimah, ***ʿĀʾishah bint Ḥanīf Abrahams.*** She informed me that she read the Minor 10 *Qirāʾāt* via the *Shāṭibiyyah* and the *Durrah*, the Major 10 *Qirāʾāt* via the *Ṭayyibah*, as well as the Four *Shādhdh* (extra-canonical) *Qirāʾāt* to Sheikh ***ʿAbd Allah ibn Ṣāliḥ al-ʿUbayd.*** He gave her *ijāzah* for all the *Qirāʾāt* and books that she read to him, as well as *ijāzah ʿāmmah*. Sheikh ʿAbd Allah al-ʿUbayd read the Minor 10 *Qirāʾāt* to Sheikhah ***Umm al-Saʿd.***

***[A closer link to the Sheikhah]:*** I read the narration of Ḥafṣ to Sheikh ***ʿAbd Allah ibn Ṣāliḥ al-ʿUbayd***, who in turn read it – incorporated within the 10 *Qirāʾāt* – to Sheikhah ***Umm al-Saʿd.***

***In Texts:*** I transmit the *Shāṭibiyyah* and the *Durrah* via *ijāzah* from Sheikh ***ʿAbd Allah al-ʿUbayd***, who read it – in its entirety – to Sheikhah ***Umm al-Saʿd.***

# 3

## *Sheikhah Nafīsah bint Abū al-ʿIlā*

1874-1954

Her name is Nafīsah bint Abū al-ʿIlā[5] ibn Aḥmad ibn Rajab. She was born in Alexandria in 1294/1874. She had memorised the Qurʾān at a very young age. Thereafter, she embarked on memorising the *Tuḥfah* of Sheikh Sulaymān Jamzūrī, the *Muqaddimat al-Jazariyyah*, the *Shāṭibiyyah* on the Seven *Qirāʾāt*, the *Durrah* on the Three remaining *Qirāʾāt*, the *Ṭayyibah* on the 10 *Qirāʾāt*, and many other texts. She then read all these *Qirāʾāt* to the *Sheikh al-Qurrāʾ* (the Grand teacher of *Qirāʾāt*) of Alexandria at that time: Sheikh ʿAbd al-ʿAzīz ʿAlī Kuḥayl.

She never married and dedicated her life to the teaching of the Qurʾān and *Qirāʾāt*. She taught from her house, passing on her knowledge of *Qirāʾāt* to whoever came to recite to her. She spent her life in this manner until she passed away, nearing the age of 80. She was a contemporary of the *Sheikh al-Qurrāʾ* of Alexandria, Sheikh Muḥammad ʿAbd al-Raḥmān al-Khalījī.

---

5. *Imtāʿ al-Fuḍalāʾ bi Tarājim al-Qurrāʾ*: 5/132.

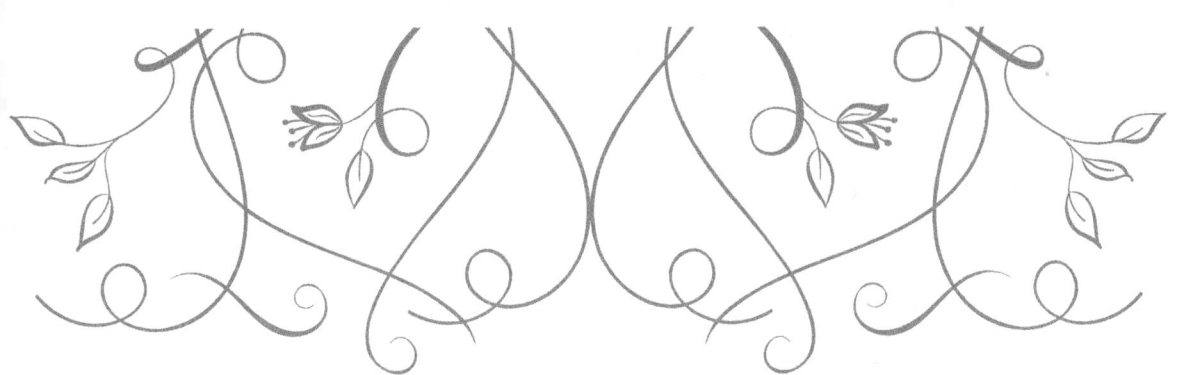

**Teachers:**

- ʿAbd al-ʿAzīz Kuḥayl.

**Students:**

- Sheikhah Umm al-Saʿd.
- Sheikh Muḥammad ʿAbd al-Ḥamīd al-Iskandarī.

She died in 1374/1954.

### My Link to Sheikhah Nafīsah bint Abū al-ʿIlā

Through my previously mentioned links to Sheikhah ***Umm al-Saʿd***, who had read and transmitted from Sheikhah ***Nafīsah***.

# 4

## *Sheikhah Nafīsah bint ʿAbd al-Karīm Zīdān*

1928-2008

Born blind in 1346/1928, Cairo, she started memorising the Qurʾān at the hands of Sheikh Muḥammad Saʿīd al-Farrāsh at the age of seven.[6] Thereafter, she memorised the *Shāṭibiyyah* and read the Seven *Qirāʾāt* to Sheikh Farrāsh.[7] One day after praying the *ʿAṣr* Prayer at the mosque of ʿAmr ibn al-ʿĀṣ, Sheikhah Hānī advised her to study the 10 *Qirāʾāt.* She then embarked on memorising the *Durrah* and read its 10 *Qirāʾāt* to Sheikh Nadā ʿAlī Nadā, a student of ʿAbd al-Fattāḥ Hunaydī.

After completing the 10 *Qirāʾāt* via the *Durrah*, she memorised the *Ṭayyibah* and read its 10 *Qirāʾāt* to Sheikh Aḥmad ʿAbd al-ʿAzīz al-Zayyāt. Her thirst for knowledge still remained unquenched, and so she read the Four *Shādhdh Qirāʾāt* to Sheikh Ḥanafī al-Saqqā.

---

6. *Imtāʿ al-Fuḍalāʾ bi Tarājim al-Qurrāʾ*: 5/135.
7. He was a student of Aḥmad al-Bardīsī, who read to Muṣṭafā Manṣūr al-Bājūrī, a student of ʿAlī Subayʿ and Muḥammad Makkī Naṣr al-Juraysī, the author of *Nihāyat al-Qawl al-Mufīd fī ʿIlm al-Tajwīd.*

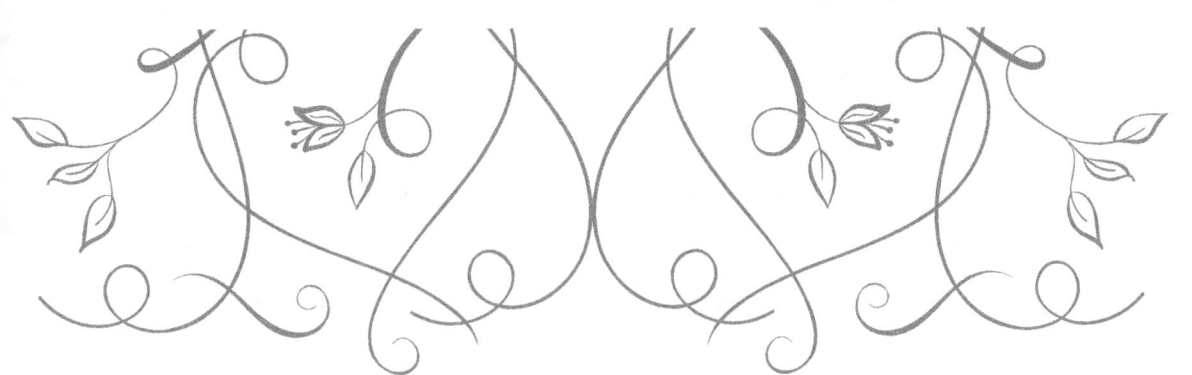

**Teachers:**

- Sheikh Muḥammad Saʿīd al-Farrāsh – she read the Seven *Qirāʾāt* via the *Shāṭibiyyah* to him. This is a unique *sanad* because it links up with the author of *Nihāyat al-Qawl al-Mufīd*, Sheikh Muḥammad Makkī Naṣr al-Juraysī. There are not many *asānīd* linked to him.
- Nadā ʿAlī Nadā – she read the 10 *Qirāʾāt* via the *Shāṭibiyyah* and the *Durrah* to him. He was a contemporary of the famous Sheikh ʿAḥmad ʿAbd al-ʿAzīz al-Zayyāt, because they both read to the same teacher, ʿAbd al-Fattāḥ Hunaydī.
- Sheikh Aḥmad ʿAbd al-ʿAzīz al-Zayyāt – she read the 10 *Qirāʾāt* via the *Ṭayyibah* to him.
- Sheikh Ḥanafī al-Saqqā – she read the Four *Shādhdh Qirāʾāt* to him and was of the last students who transmitted from him.[8]

**Students:**

- Ḥasan Muṣṭafā al-Warrāqī – he read many texts of *Tajwīd* and *Qirāʾāt* to her, as well as a portion of the Qurʾān according to the Minor 10 *Qirāʾāt* and the Major 10 *Qirāʾāt* via the *Shāṭibiyyah*, the *Durrah*, and the *Ṭayyibah.* He also read of the Four *Shādhdh Qirāʾāt* via *al-Fawāʾid al-Muʿtabarah* to her. He received *ijāzah* for everything he read to her.

She died on 9 Shaʿbān 1429/11 August 2008.

8. The other person who transmitted the Four *Shādhdh Qirāʾāt* from Sheikh al-Saqqā was Sheikh Ibrāhīm al-Samannūdī.

## My Link to Sheikhah Nafīsah bint ʿAbd al-Karīm Zīdān

***In Qurʾān:*** I read the Seven *Qirāʾāt* via the *Shāṭibiyyah* to my teacher, Sheikh ***Salīm Gaibie.*** He informed me that he read until Sūrah Āl ʿImrān combining the Minor 10 *Qirāʾāt* to Sheikh ***Ḥasan Muṣṭafā al-Warrāqī.*** He read a portion of the Qurʾān in the Minor 10 *Qirāʾāt*, the Major 10 *Qirāʾāt* as well as the Four *Shādhdh Qirāʾāt* to Sheikhah ***Nafīsah.*** He also read various texts of *Tajwīd* and *Qirāʾāt* to her. She gave him *ijāzah* for everything he read to her.

***In Texts:*** With the previously mentioned *sanad* to Sheikhah ***Nafīsah Zīdān***, I transmit the *Jazariyyah* and the *Shāṭibiyyah*, amongst various other texts in *Tajwīd* and *Qirāʾāt*.

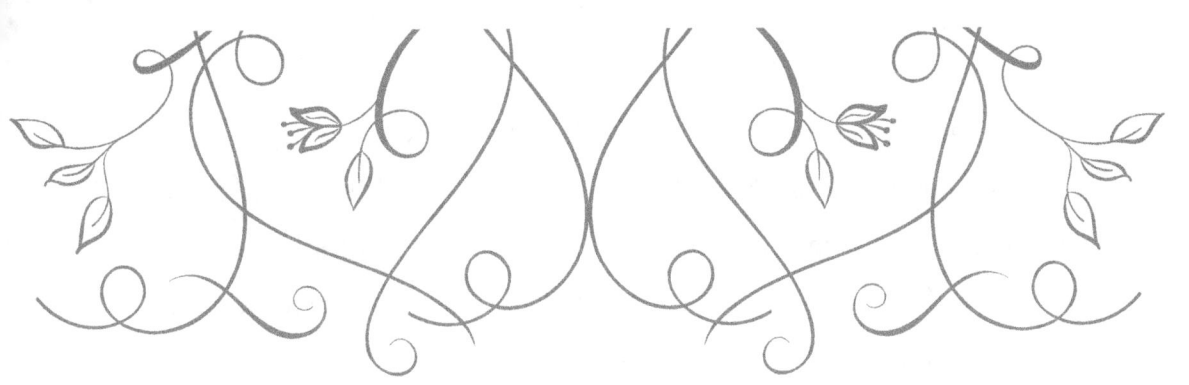

# 5

## *Sheikhah Samīʿah Muḥammad Bakr al-Bināsī*

1930-2020

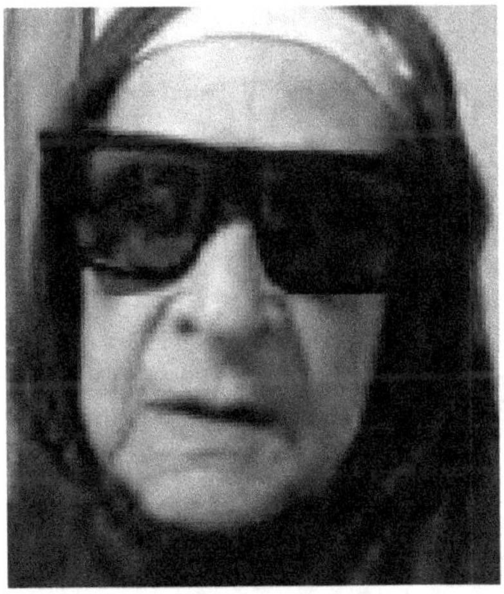

Sheikhah Samīʿah Muḥammad Sayyid Bakr al-Bināsī was born on the 18th of May, 1930, in the village of Abnahs, situated in the city of Quweisna in Monufia, Egypt.

She was born into a family who loved the Qurʾān. It is mentioned that her father memorised the Qurʾān at the hands of Sheikh Sayyid Bakr, who was from the same village. Thereafter, her father perfected his recitation with the guidance of Sheikh Maḥmūd al-ʿAnūsī, the father of Sheikhah Samīʿah's teacher.

Sheikhah Samīʿah's father yearned that one of his daughters would memorise the Qurʾān. It was the divine decree of Allah that He accepted Muḥammad Sayyid Bakr's daughter, Sheikhah Samīʿah, to memorise the Qurʾān and be included amongst His family, the *Ahl al-Qurʾān* (the fraternity of the Qurʾān).

Sheikhah Samīʿah was born blind. Though she was physically blind, Allah bestowed her with the gift of spiritual insight. She started memorising the Qurʾān at the age of six. At the age of 11, she completed her memorisation of the Qurʾān at the hands of Sheikh ʿAlī Ḥimād Māḍī, under whose guidance she also studied the *Tuḥfah* of Sheikh Jamzūrī, the *Jazariyyah,* and other texts of *Tajwīd.*

Her uncle, Sheikh Ibrahīm Mursī al-Banāsī, was one of the renowned Qurʾānic teachers, originally from her village. One of his students was none other than the famous *Sheikh al-Qurrāʾ* of Egypt during that time, Sheikh ʿĀmir Sayyid ʿUthmān. Sheikh Ibrāhīm Mursī would visit Abnahs every year for a period of three months, travelling all the way from the east of Egypt to their small village.

Her father, Muḥammad Sayyid Bakr, seized this opportunity and presented her to Sheikh Ibrahīm Mursī, to remain under his expertise.

*A student reciting to Sheikhah Samīʿah*

Sheikhah Samīʿah perfected the discipline of *Tajwīd* under his tutelage. While under his skillful guidance, she also revised her memorisation of the Qurʾān and the many texts which she had committed to memory. It was her long-term goal to someday extend her studies beyond that which she had grasped from her uncle and teacher, Sheikh Ibrāhīm.

To fulfill this goal, she later travelled to Sheikh Muṣṭafā Maḥmūd Shāhīn al-ʿAnūsi in 1948. She read the narrations of Ḥafṣ and Warsh to him, as well as the *Qirāʾah* of Ḥamzah.

Sheikh Muṣṭafā al-ʿAnūsi[9] lived in another village of Quweisna, Shubra Bakhoum. Transport between the two villages was extremely difficult. Enduring this challenging journey, she would travel to Sheikh Muṣṭafā mounted on a donkey. She would stay in Shubra Bakhoum from Saturday to Wednesday. Other students who travelled from far to study with the Sheikh would stay in a nearby house. However, Sheikh Muṣṭafā would not have that for her and arranged with her father that she stay in the Sheikh's own home, amongst his wives and children. Her father prepared whatever provisions she might require during her stay with her teacher.

Sheikhah Samīʿah was blessed with a sweet and beautiful voice. Other females loved listening to her recitation. The people of her village and

---

9. Sheikh Muṣṭafā ibn Maḥmūd al-ʿĀnūsī was born on the 9th of August, 1884, in Shubra Bakhoum. He was born and raised in a home where the Qurʾān was consistently being recited. His father took an active interest in him memorising the Qurʾān until he completed it in his childhood. He continued learning in this manner until he studied the Seven and 10 *Qirāʾāt* under his father's expertise.

   Sheikh Muṣṭafā al-ʿĀnūsī and some of his family members established one of the first official madrasahs for the memorisation of the Qurʾān and other Qurʾānic studies in the year 1906. It eventually blossomed into a primary school and a centre for Qurʾānic studies, specializing in *Tajwīd* and *Qirāʾāt*.

   Many people and children in his village and neighbouring villages studied various Qurʾānic sciences by him, including some famous reciters, like Sheikh Maḥmūd ibn Sībaway al-Badawī.

   He passed away in October 1970 and is buried in Shubra Bakhoum.

other neighbouring villages would invite her to recite in female gatherings. On occasion, some women persisted that she recite over a loudspeaker. Her recitation was so enchanting that nearby men started inquiring about her.

The Sheikhah used to say that with the grace of Allah, she was the first woman who did away with the innovation of women who would mourn as a profession.[10]

She dedicated her life to the learning and teaching of the Qurʾān. She maintained a good relationship with all her students, showering them with much affection as if they were her own children. Even though she never married, she considered her many students as her children. She gave *ijāzah* to many; women and men. Sheikhah Samīʿah passed away at almost 90 years of age in August 2020.

Sheikhah Samīʿah was considered to be from the same generation as Sheikh ʿĀmir Sayyid ʿUthmān in that she read to his teacher, Sheikh Abū Bakr Mursī al-Banāsī. Her link via Sheikh al-ʿAnūsī is also one of the shortest links to Sheikh Muṣṭafā al-Mīhī, who was the axis of the *asānīd* of *Qirāʾāt* in Tanta. Therefore, many aspired to have her *asānīd* and travelled from far and wide to recite to her.

**Teachers:**

- Sheikh ʿAlī Ḥimād Māḍī – she memorised the Qurʾān by him. She also studied and memorised the *Tuḥfah*, the *Jazariyyah*, and various other texts of *Tajwīd* by him.
- Sheikh Ibrahīm Mursī al-Banāsī – she perfected her *Tajwīd* by him. She

10. This was a service where people could hire women to professionally mourn at burials or other sad occasions on behalf of the bereaved families.

revised the Qur'ān and the various *Tajwīd* texts that she had memorised by him.

- Sheikh Muṣṭafā Maḥmūd Shāhīn al-ʿAnūsī – she recited the narrations of Ḥafṣ, Warsh, and the *Qirā'ah* of Ḥamzah to him.

**Students:**

- Sheikh Ḥasan Muṣṭafā al-Warrāqī – he read a portion of the Qur'ān to her, swapping between the narrations of Ḥafṣ, Warsh, and the *Qirā'ah* of Ḥamzah.
- Sheikh Saʿīd ibn Ṣāliḥ Zaʿīmah – he received *ijāzah* from the Sheikhah.

**My Link to Sheikhah Samīʿah**

***In Qur'ān:*** I read the Seven *Qirā'āt* via the *Shāṭibiyyah* to my teacher, Sheikh ***Salīm Gaibie.*** He informed me that he read until Sūrah Āl ʿImrān combining the Minor 10 *Qirā'āt* to Sheikh ***Ḥasan Muṣṭafā al-Warrāqī.*** He read a portion of the Qur'ān in the narrations of Ḥafṣ, Warsh, and the *Qirā'ah* of Ḥamzah to Sheikhah ***Samīʿah.*** She gave him *ijāzah* in these transmissions and *Qirā'āt*. She also gave him *ijāzah* for the *Tuḥfah* of Sheikh Jamzūrī and the *Muqaddimat al-Jazariyyah.*

***In Texts:*** Besides the above link via Sheikh ***Salīm Gaibie,*** I also heard the entire *Jazariyyah* being read in an aural audition to Sheikh Dr. ***Saʿīd ibn Ṣāliḥ Zaʿīmah*** and received *ijāzah* in it from him. Sheikh ***Zaʿīmah*** received *ijāzah* for it from Sheikhah ***Samīʿah.***

# 6

## *Sheikhah Tanādhur Muḥammad Muṣṭafā al-Najūlī*

1924-2021

Sheikhah Tanādhur was born in 1924 in the village of Nasiriyah, Samannoud, in the Gharbiyyah province of Egypt. She lost her sight when she was afflicted with measles while she was still quite young. Though she was blind, she was a woman endowed with divine insight. She portrayed the character of the *Ahl al-Qur'ān* – the fraternity of Allah – one graced with much humility and noble character.

Sheikhah Tanādhur combined the 10 *Qirā'āt*. She perfected it and subsequently devoted herself to teaching the Qur'ān for 70 years, seeking nothing but Allah's pleasure. The size of her room did not exceed two-by-two meters. Yet, this did not prevent her from opening her simple home for the study of the Noble Qur'ān. The humble room was filled to capacity with students that gathered to recite to her and listen to her. She would sit on a mat and listen attentively and tirelessly to whoever read to her. When anyone was reciting to her, she was alert and completely focused, listening full-heartedly to their reciting. The Sheikhah was brilliant, smart, and quick-witted. Even at the old age of 90, her mind was as sharp as ever when listening to her students.

Sheikhah Tanādhur mentioned that she began memorising the Qur'ān without *Tajwīd* with Sheikh ʿAbd al-Laṭīf Abū Ṣāliḥ. Then she went to Sheikh Muḥammad Abū Ḥalāwah and learned *Tajwīd* under him. She remained under his tutelage for 15 years, perfecting her recitation of the Qur'ān. She read the Seven *Qirā'āt* until Sūrah Yūnus ﷺ to him. Thereafter, she went to Sheikh Sayyid ʿAbd al-Jawwād and read the Seven *Qirā'āt* via the *Ṭarīq* of the *Shāṭibiyyah*, and subsequently, the *Qirā'āt* in the *Durrah* to him until Sūrat al-Tawbah.

Sheikhah Tanādhur was an expert in the sciences of *Tajwīd* and *Qirā'āt*. She was a contemporary to the great Sheikh Ibrāhīm al-Samannūdī, both sharing the same teacher, Sheikh Sayyid ʿAbd al-Jawwād. Thus, after the demise of Sheikh Ibrāhīm al-Samannūdī, she was the last link – the last living student – to Sheikh Sayyid ʿAbd al-Jawwād. Due to her ex-

*The house of Sheikhah Tanādhur*

pertise and the uniqueness of her *sanad*, people from all over the world travelled to recite the Qur'ān to her; to gain from her expertise and be connected to her unique chain of transmission.

Sheikah Tanādhur married her neighbour and bore six children: four sons and two daughters. The Sheikhah lived till approximately 98 years of age. She passed away on a Saturday, 9th January 2021.

The Sheikhah passed away in the very humble house that she was born in. May Allah have mercy on Sheikhah Tanādhur and bless her. May the Qur'ān be a means of light for her, a companion to her, and may all her efforts serve as a continuous charity on her behalf.

**Teachers:**

- Sheikh ʿAbd al-Laṭīf – she memorised a portion of the Qur'ān by this Sheikh.
- Sheikh Muḥammad Abū Ḥalāwah – she studied *Tajwīd* and perfected

*A student reciting to Sheikhah Tanādhur*

her recitation of the Qur'ān by him. She spent more than 15 years under his tutelage and also read the Seven *Qirā'āt* to him until Sūrah Yūnus ﷺ.

- Sheikh Sayyid ʿAbd al-Jawwād – she read the 10 *Qirā'āt* via the *Shāṭibiyyah* and the *Durrah* to him.

**Students:**

- Sheikh Saʿīd ibn Sāliḥ Za'īmah.
- Sheikh Yaḥyā al-Ghawthāni.
- Sheikh Muḥammad Salīm Gaibie.

### My Link to Sheikhah Tanādhur

***In Qur'ān:*** I read the Seven *Qirā'āt* via the *Shāṭibiyyah* to my teacher, Sheikh ***Salīm Gaibie***. He informed me that he read Sūrat al-Fātiḥah and the first five verses of Sūrat al-Baqarah combining the Seven *Qirā'āt* to Sheikhah ***Tanādhur***. She gave him *ijāzah* in the Seven *Qirā'āt* and for all her transmissions.

***In Texts:*** I heard the entire *Jazariyyah* being read to Sheikh Dr. ***Saʿīd ibn Ṣāliḥ Zaʿīmah*** and received *ijāzah* in it from him. Sheikh ***Zaʿīmah*** received *ijāzah ʿammah* from Sheikhah ***Tanādhur***.

# 7

## *Sheikhah Kareema Carol Czerepinski*

She is Sheikhah Kareema[11] bint Henry Peter Czerepinski. Her birth name was Carol Czerepinski, but she later used the name Kareema when she reverted to Islam. Sheikhah Kareema was born on 13 Jumād al-Ūlā 1376/15 December 1956 in Madison City, Wisconsin, in the United States of America.

She grew up and studied in Madison City, graduating from High School with distinction in 1395/1975. Thereafter, she enrolled at the University of Wisconsin, receiving her Bachelor's degree in natural remedies in 1399/1979. The next two years saw her working in this specialised field. During this period, she read certain books on Islam and subsequently became a Muslim. She married and later moved to Jeddah in the Kingdom of Saudi Arabia in 1401/1981, where she worked in one of the military hospitals. She became engrossed in her studies of Islam through the available English literature at the time and stopped working at the hospital.

A major turning point in the life of this Qur'ānic teacher was when she read about the great virtues and rewards attached to those who dedicate

11. *Imtāʿ al-Fuḍalāʾ bi Tarājim al-Qurrāʾ*: 5/75.

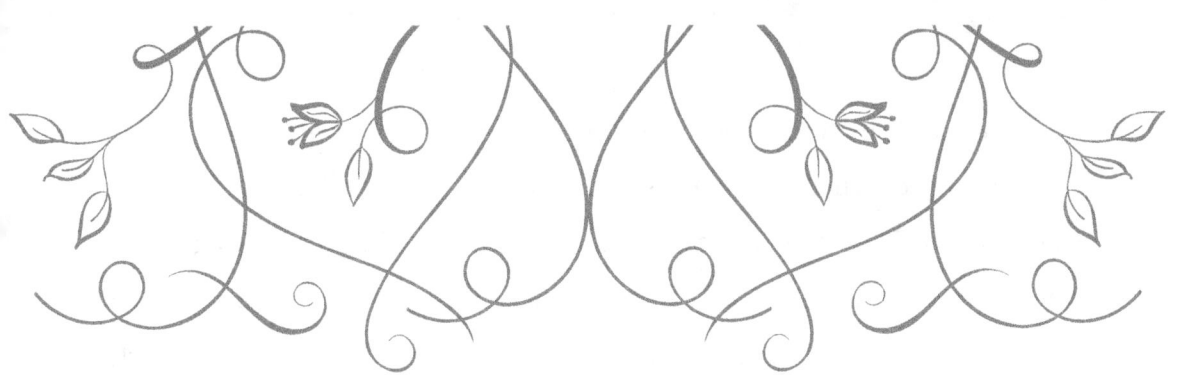

their lives to the memorisation and teaching of the Qur'ān. She then embarked on the journey of memorising the Qur'ān as well as studying the rules of *Tajwīd*, which lasted for a period of seven years. During this time, Sheikhah Kareema also studied many of the authentic classical works on *Tajwīd* and *Qirā'āt*, as well as rendering all 10 *Qirā'āt* via the *Ṭarīq* of the *Shāṭibiyyah* and the *Durrah* to a qualified teacher.

Sheikhah Kareema presently heads a department for non-Arabic speaking women at Madrasah Dār al-Hudā in Jeddah. She is the author of the famous book series *Tajweed Rules of the Quran* and also oversees the website *About Tajweed,*[12] which teaches as well as answers many questions in the sciences of *Tajwīd* and *Qirā'āt*. We pray that Allah gives her a long life with many good deeds and increases her in piety and knowledge.

**Teachers:**

- Sheikhah Riḥāb Muḥammad Mufīd Shaqaqī, the wife of Sheikh Dr. Ayman Rushdī Suwayd – she read to her and received *ijāzah* in the narration of Ḥafṣ via the *Shāṭibiyyah* and the *Ṭayyibah,* as well as the 10 *Qirā'āt* via the *Shāṭibiyyah* and the *Durrah.*

**Students:**

- Mu'allimah 'Ā'ishah Abrahams – she read the entire *Muqaddimat al-Jazariyyah* to her in one sitting when she visited Cape Town.
- Sheikh Salīm Gaibie – he read all three volumes of her book, *Tajweed Rules of the Quran,* to her. He was the first to receive *ijāzah* from her in these books.

12. www.abouttajweed.com

## My Link to Sheikhah Kareema

***In Texts:*** I read *al-Muqaddimat al-Jazariyyah* from memory in one sitting, as well as selected sections from the poem, *al-Mufīd fī al-Tajwīd*, of Sheikh Aḥmad al-Ṭībī to my Muʿallimah, ***ʿĀʾishah bint Ḥanīf Abrahams.*** She informed me that she read it to Sheikhah ***Kareema.***

***In Texts:*** I studied and read *Tajweed Rules of the Quran* – all three volumes – to my teacher, Sheikh ***Salīm Gaibie,*** who read all three volumes to the author, Sheikhah ***Kareema Carol Czerepinski.***

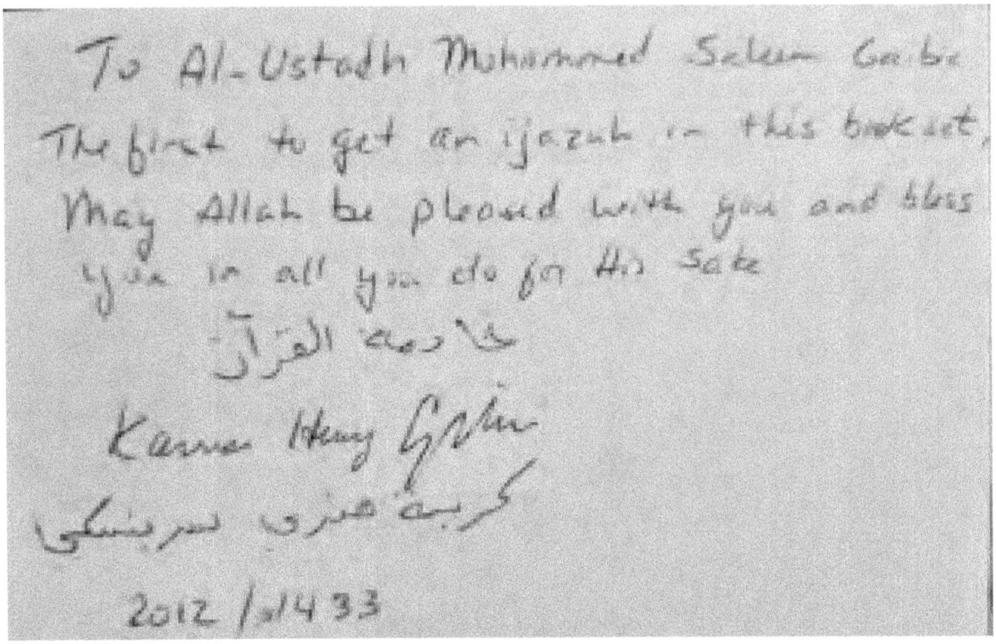
To Al-Ustadh Muhammed Saleem Gaibie
The first to get an ijazah in this book set,
May Allah be pleased with you and bless
you in all you do for His sake
خادمة القرآن
Kareema Henry
2012 / 1433

*Sheikh Salīm Gaibie's ijāzah from Sheikhah Kareema*

# 8

## *Sheikhah Riḥāb Shaqaqī*

She is Umm ʿUmar Riḥāb bint Muḥammad Mufīd ibn Fāris Shaqaqī, the wife of Sheikh Dr. Ayman Suwayd. Though her origin lies in Syria, she was born in Jeddah, Saudi Arabia, on 10 November 1973.

After completing her primary and secondary schooling in Jeddah, she enrolled in the Arabic Language Division in the Faculty of Arts at the University of Beirut for further studies. In 1996, she graduated from the university.

Sheikhah Riḥāb then studied at Dār al-Hudā in Jeddah, where she memorised the Qurʾān and mastered *Tajwīd*. This feat was followed by her studying and mastering the 10 *Qirāʾāt* at the hands of senior teachers in Egypt. It was to no surprise that she later became a teacher of *Tajwīd* and *Qirāʾāt* at the very institute where she initially studied, Dār al-Hudā.

She enrolled for higher studies at a university in America and received her doctorate due to her study and editing of *al-Tabṣirah* by Ibn Fāris al-Khayyāṭ.

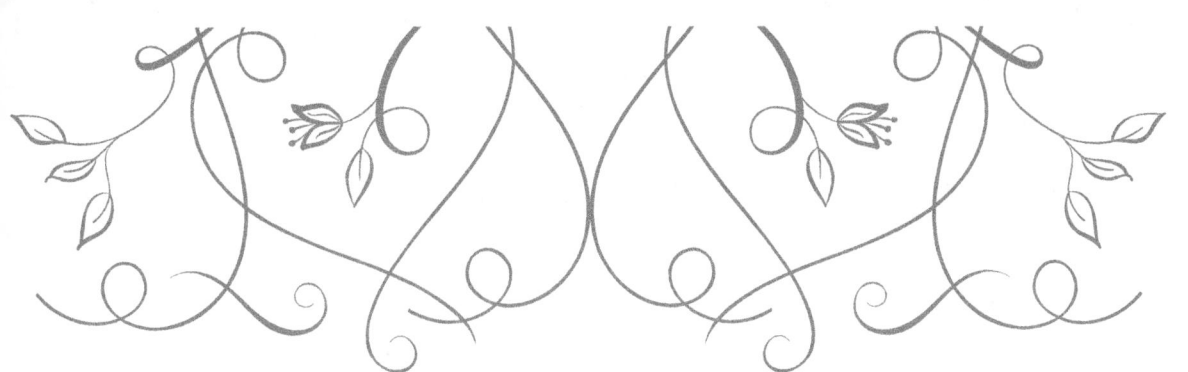

**Written works:**

*Ḥilyat al-Tilāwah fī Tajwīd al-Qurʾān.*

**Teachers:**

- Rāwiyah Ḥamdī Gharābah – she studied *Tajwīd* by her.
- Sheikh Dr. Ayman Rushdī Suwayd – she read the narration of Ḥafṣ to him twice, first via the *Shāṭibiyyah* and then via the *Ṭayyibah*. She then read a third *khatm* in the 10 *Qirāʾāt* via the *Shāṭibiyyah* and the *Durrah* and subsequently a fourth *khatm* in the 10 *Qirāʾāt* via the *Ṭayyibah*. She also studied the *Jazariyyah*, the *Shāṭibiyyah*, the *Durrah*, the *Ṭayyibah*, the *ʿAqīlah*, *Nāṭḥimat al-Zuhr*, *Talkhīṣ Ṣarīḥ al-Naṣṣ* of Sheikh ʿAbd al-ʿAzīz ʿUyūn al-Sūd, and *Manṭḥūmat al-Mufīd* of al-Ṭībī.
- Sheikh ʿĀdil al-Ḥimṣī – she read a portion of the Qurʾān to him in the 10 *Qirāʾāt* via the *Ṭayyibah* and read sections of the *Ṭayyibah* to him. She received *ijāzah* for everything she read to him.
- Ibrāhīm al-Samannūdī – she read a portion of the Qurʾān in the 10 *Qirāʾāt* via the *Shāṭibiyyah* and the *Durrah* to him. She also read sections of the *Jazariyyah*, the *Shāṭibiyyah*, the *Durrah*, the *Ṭayyibah*, and his book, *Laʾāliʾ al-Bayān*. She received *ijāzah* from him in all this as well his all his written works.

**Students:**

- Kareema Carol Czerepinski.

## My Link to Sheikhah Riḥāb

***In Texts:*** I read *al-Muqaddimat al-Jazariyyah* from memory in one sitting, as well as selected sections from the poem, *al-Mufīd fī al-Tajwīd*, of Sheikh

Aḥmad al-Ṭībī to my Muʿallimah, ***ʿĀʾishah bint Ḥanīf Abrahams.*** She informed me that she read it to Sheikhah ***Kareema***, who read these works to Sheikhah ***Riḥāb Shaqaqī.***

# 9

## *Sheikhah Amat-Allah bint ʿAbd al-Ghanī al-Dihlawī*

1835-1938

She is Amat-Allah[13] bint ʿAbd al-Ghanī bin Abī Saʿīd Aḥmad bin ʿAbd al-ʿAzīz bin ʿĪsā al-ʿUmariyyah.

She was born in Medina on the 16th of Shaʿbān 1251/6 December 1835. Sheikhah Amat-Allah benefitted from a good upbringing in the house of the well-known *muḥaddith*, her father, Sheikh ʿAbd al-Ghanī bin Abū Saʿīd al-Mujaddidī al-Madanī.

Her father initiated her learning by teaching her the Qurʾān and some fundamental classes of *dīn*. Then she learned some Ḥanafī *fiqh* books under him, as well as *Naḥw*, *Ṣarf*, and *Adab*.

Thereafter, she took an interest in the studies of hadith, eventually succeeding her father after his passing. Sheikhah Amat-Allah studied the six canonical books of hadith on many occasions with her father, either by her reading it to him or by others reading it to him. She also read many shorter texts as well as *athbāt* (a curriculum vitae of a scholar's Islamic pedigree; which documents an individual's teachers and transmissions).

13. *Muʿjam al-Maʿājim wa al-Mashīkhāt:* 2/443; *Tashnīf al-Asmāʿ bi Shuyūkh al-Ijāzah was al-Samāʿ*: 1/269.

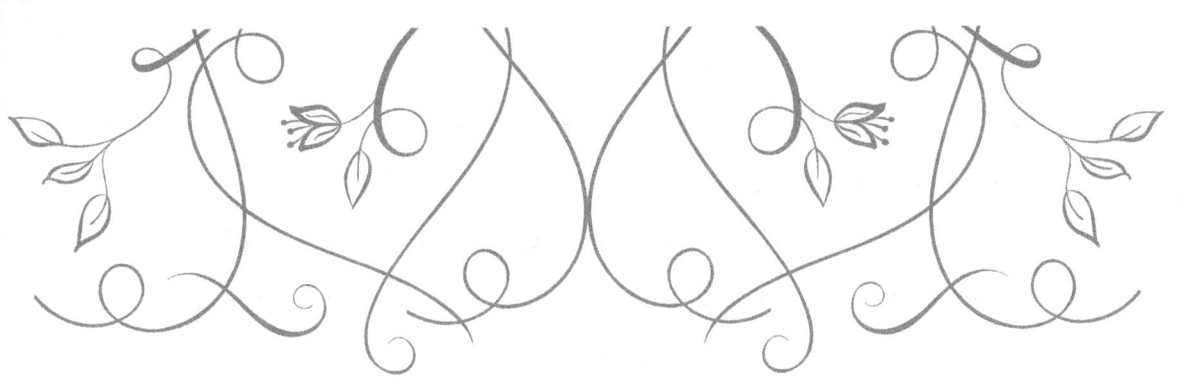

Sheikha Amat-Allah received the *musalsalāt* hadith as well as *ijāzah ʿāmmah* for her father's transmissions.

Her father took a lot of interest in her Islamic education, to such a degree that whenever he met any scholars of hadith, he would obtain *ijāzah* for Sheikhah Amat-Allah as well. He obtained *ijāzāt* for her from leading hadith scholars, including his own teachers.[14] It is for this reason that father and daughter are both documented as transmitting from the same teachers.

Sheikhah Amat-Allah took great interest in educating females regarding their religious affairs. She taught them shorter books of hadith, including books of *Fiqh*, like *Mukhataṣar al-Qudūrī.*

After her father passed away, many started seeking her out to benefit from her knowledge and high *asānīd*. Scholars would come to her home, seeking *ijāzah* from her. In most cases, they used to listen to the recitation of Sheikh Ibrahim Saʿd Allah al-Khatnī al-Madanī reading sections from different books to her, including the *Ṣaḥīḥ* of Bukhārī and the *Ṣaḥīḥ* of Muslim. She would then issue them with written *ijāzāt*

Sheikhah Amat-Allah lived for more than 100 years. She was the last one to pass away from the students of her father, Sheikh ʿAbd al-Ghanī ibn Abī Saʿīd al-Dihlawī.

After her demise, the chain of those who transmit from her father dropped by one rank, especially for the people of India, particularly their *āsānid* to Shāh ʿAbd al-Ghanī al-Dihlawī and Muḥammad ʿĀbid Sindī; all converging at the famous Shāh Waliyyullah al-Dihlawī.

Sheikhah Amat-Allah passed away in Medinah in 1357/1938. Many distinguished scholars in the world transmit from her, the likes of Sheikh

14. Sheikh Maḥmūd Saʿīd Mamdūḥ particularly mentions that this is a very high link because via Sheikhah Amat-Allah, one is linked to her father's teachers, like Sheikh Muḥammad ʿAbid Sindī (1258/1841). See *Tashnīf al-Asmāʿ bi Shuyūkh al-Ijāzah was al-Samāʿ*: 1/269.

Ibrāhīm Saʿd Allah Al-Khatnī, Sheikh Aḥmad Ghumārī, and Sheikh Muḥammad Yāsīn al-Fādānī.

### Teachers:

- Shāh ʿAbd al-Ghanī al-Dihlawī.

### Students:

- Sheikh Ibrāhīm Saʿd Allah Al-Khatnī.
- Sheikh Muḥammad Yāsīn al-Fādānī.
- ʿAbd al-Raḥmān ibn ʿAbd al-Ḥayy al-Kattānī.

### My Link to Sheikhah Amat-Allah

***In Texts:*** I received *ijāzah ʿāmmah* from the Yemeni Sheikhah, ***Ṣafiyyah bint Yaḥyā al-Ahnūmī.*** She received *ijāzah* from the *muḥaddith* of Mecca and Medina, ***ʿUmar Ḥamdān al-Maḥrasī,*** who received *ijāzah* from Sheikhah ***Amat-Allah bint ʿAbd al-Ghanī.***

***[An alternate link to the Sheikhah]:*** I received *ijāzah* from our esteemed teacher in Cape Town, the polymath, Mufti ***Muḥammad Ṭāhā Karaan.***[15] He received *ijāzah* from Sheikh ***ʿAbd al-Raḥmān ibn ʿAbd al-Ḥayy al-Kattānī,*** who received *ijāzah* from Sheikhah ***Amat-Allah bint ʿAbd al-Ghanī.***

15. While I received *ijāzah* (*riwāyah*) of hadith and other Islamic disciplines from our esteemed Mufti Ṭāhā Karaan – via *ijāzah ʿāmmah* (unrestricted *ijāzah*) for all his transmissions – I grasped his insight and knowledge (*dirāyah*) of these sciences via his student and my teacher, Muʿallimah Wardah Mohamed. She spent more than a decade studying various Islamic sciences under the tutelage of Mufti Ṭāhā and was the only female whom he taught. Muʿallimah Wardah is currently the principal of the female division of Dār al-ʿUlūm al-ʿArabiyyat al-Islāmiyyah (DUAI), Cape Town. Her profile may be found in *al-Tanzīl's Database of Sanad-Holders*. I pray that Allah allows us to continue benefitting from her and make our learning, teaching and application a continuous reward for Mufti Ṭāhā Karaan.

## The Sanad of Sheikhah Amat-Allah to Imam Bukhārī[16]

*Imam Muḥammad ibn Ismāʿīl Bukhārī (d. 256)*

*Muḥammad ibn Yūsuf Firabrī (d. 320)*

*ʿAbd Allah Ḥammūyah Sarakhsī (d. 381)*

*ʿAbd al-Raḥman ibn Muṭḥaffar Dāwūdī (d. 467)*

*Abū al-Waqt Sijzī Harawī (d. 553)*

*Ḥusayn ibn Mubārak (d. 631)*

*Abū al-ʿAbbās Aḥmad Ḥajjār (d. 730)*

*Abū Isḥāq Ibrāhīm Tanūkhī (d. 800)*

*Ibn Ḥajar ʿAsqalānī (d. 852)*

*Zakariyyā Anṣārī (d. 926)*

*Shams al-Dīn Muḥammad Ramlī (d. 1004)*

*Aḥmad ibn ʿAlī Shinnāwī (d. 1028)*

*Ṣafiyy al-Dīn Qushāshī (d. 1071)*

*Ibrāhīm ibn Ḥasan Kurdī (d. 1101)*

*Abū Ṭāhir Muḥammad Kurdi (d. 1145)*

*Shāh Waliyy Allah Dihlawī (d. 1176)*

*Shāh ʿAbd al-ʿAzīz Dihlawī (d. 1239)*

*Muḥammad Isḥāq Dihlawī (d. 1262)* *Abū Saʿīd ibn Ṣafī Dihlawī (d. 1249)*

*ʿAbd al-Ghanī ibn Abī Saʿīd (d. 1296)*

*Amat-Allah bint ʿAbd al-Ghanī (d. 1357/1938)*

*ʿAbd al-Raḥmān al-Kattānī*

*Muḥammad Ṭāhā Karaan (d. 1442/2021)*

*Gadija Bester*

16. This particular *sanad* is considered to be via aural audition (*samāʿ*) from Sheikhah Amat-Allah to Imam Bukhārī. See *Yāniʿ al-Janī min Asānīd al-Sheikh ʿAbd al-Ghanī*: 55. I have only mentioned the *sanad* to the *Ṣāḥīḥ* of Imam Bukhārī. The *asānīd* of the remaining five canonical hadith works are mentioned in the aforementioned *Yāniʿ al-Janī*.

# 10

## *Sheikhah ʿĀʾishah bint Ḥanīf Ibrāhīm*

She is ʿĀʾishah bint Ḥanīf Abrahams, more commonly referred to as Muʿallimah ʿĀʾishah. She is documented as the first female in South Africa to complete the study and recitation of the 14 *Qirāʾāt*; the Minor 10 *Qirāʾāt* via *al-Shāṭibiyyah* and *al-Durrah*, the Major 10 *Qirāʾāt* via *al-Ṭayyibah* and the Four *Shādhdh Qirāʾāt*.

She was born in the year 1993 in Wynberg, Cape Town. Muʿallimah ʿĀʾishah is the second eldest daughter of four sisters, who are also *ḥāfiṭhāt* (memorisers) of the Qurʾān. She learned how to recite the Qurʾān from her parents. At the age of 9, she started her *ḥifṭh* (memorisation) with Muʿallimah ʿĀʾishah Ceres and completed her *ḥifṭh* at the age of 14 under the tutelage of Muʿallimah Zāhidah Majiet.

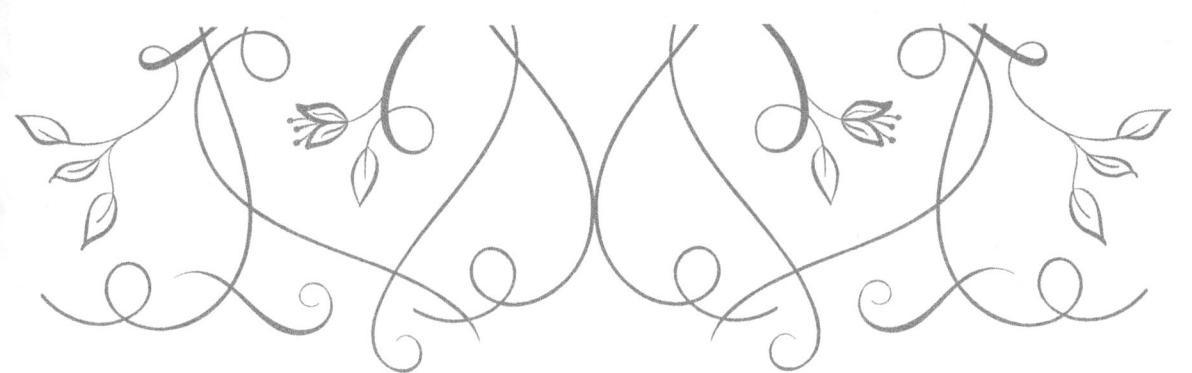

During her *ḥifṭh* journey, she attended three different schools and her *ḥifṭh* program varied from school to school. She strategically maintained a rigorous revision program by combining what was required from her at school with her own personal revision program. At school, she read an average of three *ajzāʾ* to someone, which she excluded from her personal program. Her personal program had her reading 10-12 *ajzāʾ* daily. She read the last five *ajzāʾ* every morning before class. After school, in the afternoons, she would read another 5-7 *ajzāʾ* of her memorised work.

Muʿallimah ʿĀʾishah attributes her interest and success in memorising the Qurʾān to the acceptance of the prayer (*duʿāʾ*) of the esteemed Sheikh Ṣāliḥ Abādi.[17] As a little girl, her father, Ḥanīf Abrahams ﵀, would frequent Sheikh Ṣaliḥ's company, and her grandmother would often cook meals for Sheikh Ṣaliḥ's family. At this young age, Muʿallimah ʿĀʾishah accompanied her parents to take food for the Sheikh with her parents. On numerous occasions, he would make *duʿāʾ* that Allah grants her and her sisters to become *ḥuffāṭḥ* of the Qurʾān. In this manner, growing up, their father frequently reminded them of this *duʿāʾ*, naturally encouraging them on their *ḥifṭḥ* journeys.

Muʿallimah ʿĀʾishah was intrigued by the sciences of Qurʾān and had an interest in it since she started her *ḥifṭḥ*. When she commenced reading for *ijāzah*, she realised the lack of female scholarship within the sciences of *Tajwīd* and *Qirāʾāt* in South Africa. She then set out to accomplish as much as she could in this field so that she could afford other females the opportunity of studying and reading to a female. Irrespective of which teacher she was reading to or studying with, her father accompanied her to all her classes.

17. Sheikh Ṣāliḥ ʿAbādī (25 December 1911-14 September 1999) was recognised as the doyen of the *ḥāfiṭḥ* fraternity during his time. At the age of 15, he had memorised the entire Qurʾān under the guidance of Imam Muʿāwiyah Sedick. In 1927, upon the inspiration of his father and his teacher, he left for Mecca to further his studies. In Mecca, he recited the entire Qurʾān to Sheikh Muḥammad Jamāl ibn ʿAbd al-Muʿṭī Mīrdād in the narration of Ḥafṣ via the *Ṭarīq* of *al-Shāṭibiyyah*. To the satisfaction of his teacher, he issued Sheikh Ṣāliḥ an *ijāzah* and *sanad* for the narration of Ḥafṣ. Sheikh Ṣāliḥ may be regarded as one of the first in the Cape – if not the first – to receive *ijāzah* and *sanad* in the Qurʾān, by which he is linked through a chain of teachers to the Prophet Muḥammad ﷺ. (Ed. M. Saleem Gaibie).

After completing her *ḥifṭḥ* in 2009, she enrolled in the "Qurrāʾ Development Program".[18] While enrolled in this program, her father approached Mawlana Salīm Gaibie and requested that he allow her to recite to him for *ijāzah*. Mawlana Salīm was reluctant to teach females during that time and was not too keen on allowing any females to recite to him. He made an excuse to avoid accepting her as a student and gave her father the prerequisite that she should first recite a *khatm* to one of his students; then only would he allow her to recite to him. He thought that she would not follow through and read to anyone, but a year or two later, her father again approached Mawlana Salīm and reminded him about the prerequisite he had laid down. By that time, Muʿallimah ʿĀʾishah had read a few *khatms* to Mawlana Salīm's student, Sheikh ʿAbd al-Raḥmān Davids. She had read a *khatm* in the narration of Ḥafṣ via *al-Shāṭibiyyah*, another *khatm* incorporating the *Ṭuruq* of Ḥafṣ via the *al-Ṭayyibah* and subsequently, a *khatm* in the *Qirāʾah* of Abū ʿAmr Baṣrī. Additionally, she had also studied many texts by Sheikh ʿAbd al-Raḥmān. Sheikh ʿAbd al-Raḥmān informed Mawlana Salīm that not only had she studied and understood these texts, but she had memorised them as well. In this manner, Muʿallimah ʿĀʾishah became Mawlana Salīm's first female student.

After studying the *Shāṭibiyyah* under Sheikh Ismāʿīl Londt and learning how to combine multiple *Qirāʾāt* (*jamʿ al-Qirāʾāt*), she started her first *khatm* by Mawlana Salīm in the Seven *Qirāʾāt* via *al-Shāṭibiyyah*. She also memorised the text of *al-Shāṭibiyyah* by him; the *uṣūl* and the *farsh*. Thereafter, she started reading a *khatm* in the Three *Qirāʾāt* via *al-Durrah*

18. This program taught basic Arabic, the foundational sciences for those who wished to recite the Qurʾān correctly, various traditional texts in *Tajwīd*, *Qirāʾāt*, *ʿUlūm al-Qurʾān*, Qurʾānic etiquette, etc.

to Mawlana Salīm. She had previously read these Three *Qirāʾāt* in individual *khatms* to Sheikh ʿAbd al-Raḥmān Davids; a *khatm* for Abū Jaʿfar, a *khatm* for Yaʿqūb, and a *khatm* for Khalaf al-ʿĀshir.

When asked about what Muʿallimah was particular about during the course of her studies, she responded: "writing." She used to write down everything she studied. If she struggled to remember or understand anything, she wrote it down. After every class, she would listen to the audio recording of the class and then formulate her own notes on it. In this manner, she re-wrote the *Murshid al-Qārī* book series: books one, two, and three from memory. She also penned her own commentary on *Laʾāliʾ al-Bayān* of Sheikh Samannūdī, a commentary on *al-Salsabīl al-Shāfī* of Sheikh ʿUthmān Murād, and a commentary on the *uṣūl* of *al-Shāṭibiyyah*; all during the course of studying these texts. Similarly, once she started reading the Seven *Qirāʾāt*, whatever inconsistent (*farsh*) changes she encountered during that week, she would write down in the sequence of appearance and practise it daily. She would practise reading individual narrations (*riwāyāt*) from memory by reading five *ajzāʾ* daily. After she completed a *khatm* for one *riwāyah*, she would commence another in a different *riwāyah*. She continued this practice during her study of the Minor 10 *Qirāʾāt* as well. Fridays would be her day for revision, in which she revised all the texts or books she had learned.

In 2016, her *khatm* in the Three *Qirāʾāt* to Malwana Salīm was paused because both Muʿallimah ʿĀʾishah and Mawlana Salīm had an opportunity to read the 10 *Qirāʾāt* as well as the Four *Shādhdh Qirāʾāt* to Sheikh ʿAbd Allah ibn Ṣaliḥ al-ʿUbayd during his visit to Cape Town. During this *khatm*, Mawlana Salīm heard her recite the entire Qurʾān in the Major 10

*Qirā'āt* as well as the Four *Shādhdh Qirā'āt* to Sheikh ʿUbayd. She subsequently read another independent *khatm* to Sheikh ʿUbayd in 2018. Sheikh ʿUbayd wrote two separate *ijāzahs* for her on the conclusion of each *khatm*. Mawlana Salīm also issued her with *ijāzah* because he heard her recite the entire Qur'ān in these *Qirā'āt*.

Mawlana Salīm once asked Sheikh ʿUbayd if he had any other female students who were reciting *Qirā'āt* to him. He replied that Muʿallimah ʿĀ'ishah was his first. He continued to say that in all her renditions to him, she did not falter in her recitation; she did not leave out a *wajh* (way of reading) in *Qirā'āt* nor mix their sequencing. Mawlana Salīm also acknowledges that he only recalled one place that he had asked her to repeat when she was reading the Seven *Qirā'āt* to him.

From her early years, she demonstrated great aptitude for learning and possessed unquestionable talent. Her academic excellence and achievements, coupled with dedication and consistency, distinguish her as an extraordinaire in the Qur'ānic field. Her scholarly aptitude was not only visible and admired by her local teachers but by visiting international scholars too. When Sheikh ʿAbd Allah Jār-Allah visited Cape Town in 2014,[19] he met up with Mawlana Salīm. During their discussions, Mawlana Salīm mentioned that Muʿallimah ʿĀ'ishah had memorised the famous poem of Sheikh Samannūdī, *La'āli' al-Bayān*. When Sheikh Jār-Allah heard this, he insisted to meet this student. He scheduled an appointment with her in which she read the entire *La'āli' al-Bayān* to him from memory. He gave her *ijāzah* for the text as well as for some of his own written works.

19. He recited *Qirā'āt* to many of the leading experts in the world, like Sheikh Ibrāhīm Akhḍar, Sheikh Zayyāt, Sheikh ʿAbd al-Rāfiʿ Sharqāwī, Sheikh Bakrī Tarābīshī, Sheikh Muḥammad Kurayyim Rājiḥ, Sheikh Muḥammad Tamīm al-Zuʿbī, and Sheikh Abū al-Ḥasan Muḥy al-Dīn al-Kurdī. He is also considered the last student of the famous Sheikh Ibrāhīm Samannūdī. See *Imtāʿ al-Fuḍalā'*: 1/258.

On another occasion, Sheikh Aḥmad Saʿd al-Azharī met her and tested her reading on various *riwāyāt*; Warsh, Khalaf, and Khallād, in particular. She subsequently read the entire *Tuḥfat al-Aṭfāl* and *Muqaddimat al-Jazariyyah* to him from memory. He read the entire *Salsabīl al-Shāfī* to her, amongst a few *musalsalāt* hadith, and gave her *ijāzah*. She also had the opportunity to read the *Muqaddimat al-Jazariyyah*, along with other minor texts, to Sheikhah Kareema Czerepinski.

Muʿallimah ʿĀʾishah's careful attention to detail is something that stands out to her teachers and students. All her students can attest to her scrupulous nature; her ears always attuned to the recitation of the Qurʾān and her mind alert to any discussions about it. Whenever asked about any matter of *Tajwīd* or *Qirāʾāt*, she always had the answers at her fingertips, answering confidently and precisely.

In addition to her completing four years study of Higher Islāmic Studies at Dār al-Naʿīm in 2015, she acquired a BA Honours degree in religion and theology from the University of the Western Cape.

It is not only her achievements and proficiency as a teacher that makes her exceptional, but her character and graceful nature, which manifests in her patience and tolerance when dealing with her students. When correcting them, she would calmly guide them in the correct direction, patiently waiting for them to answer correctly, regardless of how many mistakes they made. There is never a sign of agitation or frustration from her.

**Teachers:**[20]

- Mu'allimah 'Ā'ishah Ceres – started *ḥifṭḥ* of the Qur'ān by her.
- Mu'allimah Zāhidah Majiet – completed *ḥifṭḥ* of the Qur'ān by her.
- Mawlana 'Ali Goder – studied *Naḥw, Tarjamah, Mīrāth* and *'Aqidah* by him.
- Mawlana Salīm Gaibie – studied the *Jazariyyah, al-La'ali' al-Bayān, al-Salsabīl al-Shāfī, Uṣul al-Qirā'āt*, and the textbooks of Sheikhah Kareema Carol Czerepinski – *Tajweed Rules of the Quran* – by him. She also memorised the *Shāṭibiyyah* as well as completed a *khatm* in the Seven *Qirā'āt* by him. She received *ijāzah* in all 14 *Qirā'āt* from him after rendering all these *Qirā'āt* to Sheikh 'Abd Allah ibn Ṣāliḥ al-'Ubayd in the presence of Mawlana Salīm.
- Sheikh 'Abd al-Raḥmān Davids – recited the narration of Ḥafṣ and Shu'bah via the *Shāṭibiyyah*, the narration of Ḥafṣ via the *Ṭayyibah*, the narration of Qālūn, the *Qirā'ah* of Abū 'Amr Baṣrī and the *Qirā'ah* of Abū Ja'far to him. Also studied *Murshid al-Qāri* (Book 1), the *Tuḥfah, Bahjat al-Luḥḥaṭḥ*, the text of Sheikh 'Āmir 'Uthmān and *Tawḍīḥ al-Ma'ālim li Ṭuruq Ḥafṣ* by him.
- Sheikh Isma'īl Londt – studied *Ṣarf* and *'Ulūm al-Qur'ān* by him. Completed the study of the *uṣūl* of the *Shāṭibiyyah* by him.
- Sheikh Iḥsān Davids – studied *Murshid al-Qāri* (Book 1) and the *Tuḥfah* by him. Learned how to combine the Seven *Qirā'āt* (*jam' al-qirā'āt*) by him.
- Sheikh Iḥsān Abrahams – recited 19 and a half *ajzā'* for the narration of Ḥafṣ via the *ṭarīq* of the *Rouḍah* of Mu'addil to him.

---

20. These are a list of a few of her teachers. A more comprehensive list of her teachers may be found in *al-Tanzīl's Database of Sanad-Holders.*

- Qāri Ayyūb Isḥāq – heard (*samā'*) the *Jazariyyah* being read to him. Received a written *ijāzah* from him for it.
- Sheikh Aḥmad Sa'd al-Ḥasanī al-Azharī – read sections of the Qur'ān to him in the narrations of Qālūn, Warsh, Khalaf, and the Reading of 'Āṣim, and received *ijāzah* from him.
- Dr. 'Abd Allah al-Jār Allah – read *al-La'āli' al-Bayān* of Samannūdī to him from memory and received *ijāzah* for it, as well as for some of his written works from him.
- Sheikh Abū Muḥammad Idrīs al-Shāfi'ī – read sections from *al-Tibyān fī 'Ulūm al-Qur'ān* and *Ṣafwat al-Tafāsīr* of Sheikh Muḥammad 'Alī Ṣābūnī to him and received *sanad* and *ijāzah* for them. Also read a portion of the Qur'ān to him in the narration of Ḥafṣ and received *ijāzah* from him.
- Sheikh Yaḥyā Ghouthānī – heard *Al-Arba'ūn al-Ghouthāniyyah* being read to him. Received *ijāzah* for it as well as *ijāzah 'āmmāh* from him.
- Mawlana Ṭāhā Karaan – received *ijāzah 'āmmah* from him.
- Sheikh 'Abd Allah ibn Ṣāliḥ ibn Muḥammad al-'Ubayd – completed the Ten *Qirā'āt* via the *Ṭayyibah* and the Four *Shādhdh Qirā'āt* by reading a collective *khatm* to him incorporating all these *Qirā'āt* as well as an independent *khatm*. She also read from the *Shāṭibiyyatayn*, *Naṭḥimat al-Zuhr*, *al-Durrah*, *al-Ṭayyibah*, *al-Nashr*, *al-Itḥāf*, *al-Muqni'*, *al-Bayān fī 'Add Āy al-Qur'ān* of al-Dānī, *al-Muḥkam*, *al-Muktafā fī al-Waqf wa al-Ibtidā*, *al-Taḥdīd*, *al-Urjūzat al-Munabbihah* of al-Dānī, *'Azw al-Ṭuruq* of al-Mutawallī, *Fatḥ al-Karīm*, *al-Rouḍ al-Naḍīr* of al-Mutawallī, *al-Ri'āyah*, *al-Minhāj* of al-Nawawī, *Itḥāf al-Bararah* of al-Azmīrī, *Manṭḥūmat al-Ṭībī*, and *Sharḥ Muqarrib al-Taḥrīr* of al-Khalījī to the Sheikh. Also read to him the 40 ḥadīth compilations of the Sheikh on

the virtues of the Companions and virtues of the *Ahl al-Bayt*, as well as various *musalsalāt*.[21]

- Sheikh Ṣalāḥ al-Dīn al-Ḥasanī al-Tijānī – received *sanad* and *ijāzah* in the 14 *Qirā'āt*, as well as *ijāzah ʿāmmah*, from him upon the request of Mawlana Salīm Gaibie.
- Sheikh Muḥammad Yūnus Ghalbān – received *sanad* and *ijāzah* from him after reciting *Sūrat al-Fātiḥah* and the beginning of *Sūrat al-Baqarah* to him telephonically, incorporating the Seven *Qirā'āt* via the *Shāṭibiyyah*. He gave her *ijāzah* in the Seven *Qirā'āt* as well as *ijāzah ʿāmmah*.

She also received *ijāzah ʿāmmah* from Sheikh Dr. ʿAbd al-Raḥmān Kawthar ibn Mawlana ʿĀshiq Ilāhī al-Burnī al-Bulandashahrī, Sheikh Dr. ʿAbd al-Salām Muqbil al-Majīdī, Sheikh Tawfīq Ḍamrah, and Sheikh Walīd Idrīs al-Minīsī, amongst others.

**Students:**

- Ṭāhirah Brown – completed the *Qirā'ah* of Abū ʿAmr Baṣri, read the *Tuḥfah* and the *Jazariyyah*, and received *sanad* and *ijāzah* for all that she completed with Muʿallimah ʿĀ'ishah.
- Rāḍiyah Bawa – completed the *Qirā'ah* of Abū ʿAmr Baṣri and the *Qirā'ah* of Kisā'ī by her, and received *sanad* and *ijāzah* for it.
- Anīsah Jabār – studied the poems of Sheikh Shanqīṭī and Saʿīd ʿAbd Allah for the *ṭarīq* of *Miṣbāḥ*, *Bahjat al-Luḥḥāṭḥ*, the text of Sheikh ʿĀmir

21. The *musalsalāt* that were read are *al-musalsal bi al-awwaliyyah*, *al-musalsal bi al-Shāfiʿiyyah*, *al-musalsal bi al-Ḥanābilah*, *al-musalsal bi al-ḥuffāṭḥ*, *al-musalsal bi al-Qurrā'*, *al-musalsal bi al-mujawwidīn*, *al-musalsal bi qoul "Aʿūdhu bi Allah min al-Shayṭān al-Rajīm"*, *al-musalsal bi Āyat al-Kursī*, *al-musalsal bi* Sūrat al-Ḥashr, *al-musalsal bi* Sūrat al-Ṣaff, *al-musalsal bi al-sujūd fī* al-Inshiqāq, *al-musalsal bi* Sūrat al-Kawthar, *al-musalsal bi* Sūrat al-ʿAṣr, *al-musalsal bi al-maḥabbah* and *al-musalsal bi khatm al-majlis bi al-duʿā'*.

al-Sayyid ʿUthmān, *Umniyyat al-Walhān*, *Ghunyat al-Ṭalabah* of Mawlana Salīm Gaibie, and the *Shāṭibiyyah* by her. She also read a *khatm* to her in the narration of Ḥafṣ via *al-Ṭayyibah* and subsequently, a *khatm* incorporating the Seven *Qirāʾāt* via *al-Shāṭibiyyah.*

- Fuzlin Girie – studied the *Tuḥfah* of Jamzūrī under her and read a *khatm* to her in the narration of Ḥafṣ via *al-Shāṭibiyyah* and subsequently a *khatm* incorporating all the *ṭuruq* of Ḥafṣ via *al-Ṭayyibah*, as well as Shuʿbah via *al-Shāṭibiyyah.* She also read a collective *khatm* – with Fāṭimah Parker – in the *Qirāʾah* of Ibn ʿĀmir al-Shāmī via *al-Shāṭibiyyah* to her. Furthermore, she read a collective *khatm* to her in the Seven *Qirāʾāt* via *al-Shāṭibiyyah.*
- Waṣfiyyah Altalib – studied the *Tuḥfah* of Jamzūrī by her and read a *khatm* to her in the narration of Ḥafṣ via *al-Shāṭibiyyah.*
- Karīmah Jassiem – read a *khatm* to her in the narration of Ḥafṣ via *al-Ṭayyibah* and the narration of Shuʿbah via *al-Shāṭibiyyah.* She also studied *Murshid al-Qārī* of Mawlana Salīm Gaibie, *al-Tuḥfah*, *al-Jazariyyah*, *al-Laʾāliʾ al-Bayān*, *al-Salsabīl al-Shāfī*, *Bahjat al-Luḥḥāṭḥ*, the text of Sheikh ʿĀmir al-Sayyid ʿUthmān, *Umniyyat al-Walhān*, the poems of Sheikh Shinqīṭī and Saʿīd ʿAbd Allah for the *ṭarīq* of *Miṣbāḥ*, *al-Khāqāniyyah*, *al-Nūniyyah* of al-Sakhāwī and *al-Iṣbāḥ* of Sheikh al-ʿUbayd. She studied the *uṣūl* of the Seven *Qirāʾāt* via *Ghunyat al-Ṭalabah*, and then read a *khatm* to her incorporating the Seven *Qirāʾāt* via *al- Shāṭibiyyah,* and then a *khatm* incorporating the Three *Qirāʾāt* via *al-Durrah.*
- ʿĀʾishah Hassen – read a *khatm* to her in the narration of Ḥafṣ via *al-Shāṭibiyyah*, receiving *sanad* and *ijāzah.*
- Fāṭimah Parker – read a *khatm* to her in the narration of Ḥafṣ via *al-Shāṭibiyyah*, receiving *sanad* and *ijāzah.* Subsequently read a collec-

tive *khatm* to her in the narration of Ḥafṣ via the *ṭuruq* of *al-Ṭayyibah.* She also read to her a collective *khatm* – with Fuzlin Girie – in the *Qirā'ah* of Ibn ʿĀmir al-Shāmī via *al-Shāṭibiyyah.* Furthermore, she read a collective *khatm* to her in the Seven *Qirā'āt* via *al-Shāṭibiyyah.*

- Isrā Jacobs – read a *khatm* to her in the narration of Ḥafṣ via *al-Shāṭibiyyah,* receiving *sanad* and *ijāzah.* Subsequently read a collective *khatm* to her in the narration of Ḥafṣ via the *ṭuruq* of *al-Ṭayyibah.* She also studied the *Murshid al-Qārī, al-Tuḥfah* and *al- Jazariyyah* by her. She furthermore read a collective *khatm* to her in the Seven *Qirā'āt* via *al-Shāṭibiyyah.*
- Laylah Siers – read a *khatm* to her in the narration of Ḥafṣ via *al-Shāṭibiyyah,* receiving *sanad* and *ijāzah.* She also studied the *Murshid al-Qārī, al-Tuḥfah,* and *al-Jazariyyah* by her.
- Ṣiddīqah Ahmed (located in Durban, South Africa) – read a *khatm* to her in the narration of Ḥafs via *al-Shāṭibiyyah.* Subsequently read a collective *khatm* to her in the narration of Ḥafṣ via the *ṭuruq* of *al-Ṭayyibah.* She also studied *Murshid al-Qārī, al-Tuḥfah* and *al-Jazariyyah* by her. She furthermore read a collective *khatm* to her in the Seven *Qirā'āt* via *al-Shāṭibiyyah.*
- Maryam Londt – read a *khatm* to her in the narration of Ḥafṣ via *al-Shāṭibiyyah,* receiving *sanad* and *ijāzah.*
- Ḥamīdah Parker – read a *khatm* to her in the narration of Ḥafṣ via *al-Shāṭibiyyah,* receiving *sanad* and *ijāzah.*
- Ḥafṣah Jacobs – read a *khatm* to her in the narration of Ḥafṣ via *al-Shāṭibiyyah,* receiving *sanad* and *ijāzah.* Subsequently read a collective *khatm* to her in the narration of Ḥafṣ via the *ṭuruq* of *al-Ṭayyibah.* She furthermore read a collective *khatm* to her in the Seven *Qirā'āt* via *al-Shāṭibiyyah.*

- Ta᾽siyah Hendricks – she read a collective *khatm* to Mu῾allimah in the narration of Ḥafṣ via the *ṭuruq* of *al-Ṭayyibah.*
- Āminah Hendricks – she read a collective *khatm* to Mu῾allimah in the narration of Ḥafṣ via the *ṭuruq* of *al-Ṭayyibah.* She furthermore read a collective *khatm* to her in the Seven *Qirā᾽āt* via *al-Shāṭibiyyah.*
- Rifqah Jacobs – she read a collective *khatm* to Mu῾allimah in the narration of Ḥafṣ via the *ṭuruq* of *al-Ṭayyibah.* She also read a collective *khatm* to her in the Seven *Qirā᾽āt* via *al-Shāṭibiyyah.* Subsequently, she read an independent *khatm* to her incorporating the 10 *Qirā᾽āt* via *al-Shāṭibiyyah* and *al-Durrah.*
- ῾Ā᾽ishah Alexander – she read a collective *khatm* incorporating the Seven *Qirā᾽āt* via the *Shāṭibiyyah* to Mu῾allimah and received sanad and ijāzah from her.
- Gadija Bester – read an individual *khatm* to her in the narration of Ḥafṣ via *al-Shāṭibiyyah*, receiving *sanad* and *ijāzah*. Subsequently read a collective *khatm* to her in the narration of Ḥafṣ via the *ṭuruq* of *al-Ṭayyibah.* She furthermore read a collective *khatm* to her in the Seven *Qirā᾽āt* via *al-Shāṭibiyyah.*

It is a privilege to have Mu῾allimah ῾Ā᾽ishah as our teacher. We pray that Allah accepts all her efforts and opens many more opportunities for us to learn and benefit from her. May all that she does in service of the Qur᾽ān become a continuous charity and reward for her father ﷺ.

# Conclusion

The study of Qur'ān – in any or all of its dimensions – is one of the greatest achievements in this world. Despite challenges in its acquisition, there is nothing more beautiful and enriching than studying and teaching it, and the dedication, commitment, and sacrifices of these 10 amazing Sheikhahs bears testament to that. After all, the Prophet ﷺ has highlighted the status of the person who learns and teaches the Qur'ān in multiple aḥādīth. Two such narrations are:

عَنْ عُثْمَانَ رضي الله عنه عَنِ النَّبِيِّ ﷺ قَالَ:
"خَيْرُكُمْ مَنْ تَعَلَّمَ الْقُرْآنَ وَعَلَّمَهُ"

*It is reported from 'Uthmān رضي الله عنه, that the Prophet ﷺ said:*
*"The best of you is the one who learns the Qur'ān and teaches it".*[22]

22. *Bukhārī* – ḥadīth 5027.

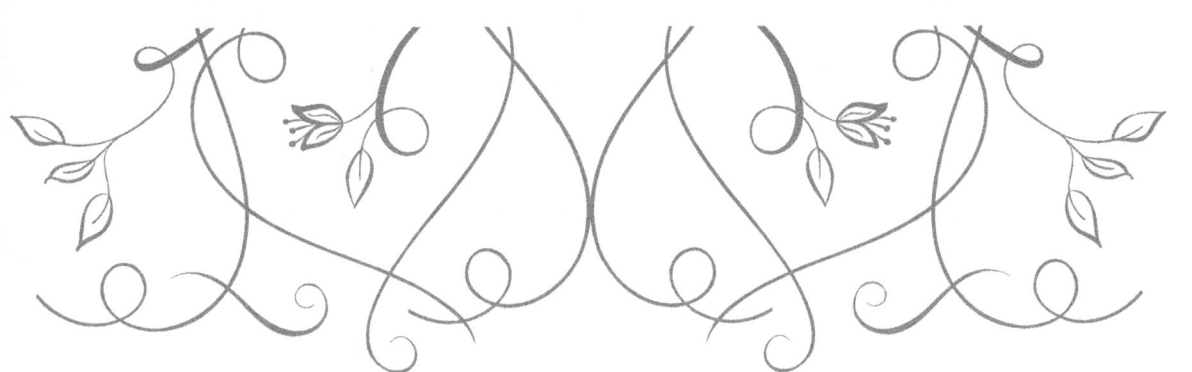

عَنْ أَنَسِ بْنِ مَالِكٍ ﵁ قَالَ: قَالَ رَسُولُ اللَّهِ ﷺ:
"إِنَّ لِلَّهِ أَهْلِينَ مِنَ النَّاسِ" قَالُوا: يَا رَسُولَ اللَّهِ، مَنْ هُمْ؟ قَالَ:
"هُمْ أَهْلُ الْقُرْآنِ، أَهْلُ اللَّهِ وَخَاصَّتُهُ"

*It is reported by Anas ibn Mālik ﵁ that the messenger of Allah ﷺ said: "Indeed, Allah has His own people amongst mankind. They (companions) said: Who are they? He ﷺ said: The fraternity of the Qur'ān is the family of Allah, specially chosen by Him."*[23]

Hence, this virtue and importance of the Qurʾān was understood by these Sheikahs and it motivated them to strive and persist in their pursuit of this beautiful endeavour, regardless of their circumstances and status.

As such, while we learn many lessons from the legacies of these Sheikhahs and while we look upon their stories with admiration, we are also reminded that we too have an opportunity to be a part of this legacy, and we have the ability to reach the potential of these women and the many other amazing female scholars of Qur'ān like them.

Allah says:

وَلَقَدْ يَسَّرْنَا ٱلْقُرْءَانَ لِلذِّكْرِ فَهَلْ مِن مُّدَّكِرٍ

*And We have certainly made the Qur'ān easy to remember. So, is there anyone who will remember? (54:22)*

23. *Sunan Ibn Mājah* – ḥadīth 215.

Allah invites all of us to pursue the study of Qurʾān and the beautiful thing about our relationship with it is that it is never too late to start, repair and aspire for more from it. In fact, its gems are unending, therefore, our efforts to study and serve the Qurʾān will forever be ongoing and unfinished. So let us accept this invitation and strive to be amongst those who the Prophet ﷺ described as the best of people, and the family of Allah ﷻ and His special people.

I make duʿā that Allah inspires and renews every reader with the zeal and sense of purpose to study the Qurʾān, through the stories of these 10 amazing Sheikahs, and that He accepts their service of the Qurʾān and that He allows their legacies to serve as pearls of perpetual wisdom for all those who endeavour to pursue it. Āmīn.

# *Epilogue*

To revere knowledge also includes revering the people of knowledge. Our rich and blessed legacy is protected by the erudite scholars who serve as the foundations of this beautiful and magnificent fortress of sacred knowledge.

Within the sanctity of the fortress, countless travellers find refuge. When the winds of tribulation threaten to uproot us, it is this fortress which fortifies us and guarantees our safety. It is thus imperative that we honour the blessed individuals whose legacy ensures our academic and spiritual development.

This book highlights the role women have always shared with men in striving to serve the Qur'an and to transmit its teachings. Within the covers of this book, we journey through the lives of ten women who represent the vast and rich female scholarship which has been interwoven within the tapestries of this din. We read this book with an intention of aspiring to this level of piety, dedication and commitment to knowledge. Additionally, we read this book with an intention that Allah favours us, our offspring and our community to be of those who walk in the footsteps of these luminaries, amin.

**MU'ALLIMAH RADIYAH BAWA**

Director of Zahraa Institute, co-founder of Goodtree Quran Foundation

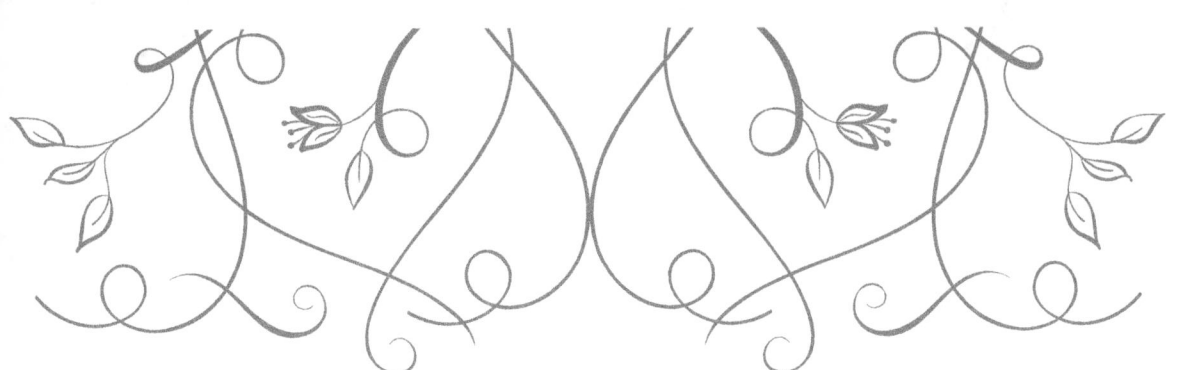

The richness of the history of the Shaykhahs, offers great insight and depth to the sacrifices made by them, in their quest of the Glorious Quraan.

This book makes it abundantly clear that the importance of the preservation of the Noble Quraan, in its different spheres, areas of studies and nuances, are the responsibility of both men and women.

I cannot aptly express my deep regard to the author, for offering us the opportunity to peek into the lives of these illustrious women, to be inspired and motivated to commit some portion of our lives to the in-depth study of the Book of Allaah. The uniqueness that I wish to share, is that the life of every woman, has an ebb and flow. We are like the moon. Ever changing. For these committed, courageous women whom Allaah had hand-picked, the challenges, I believe would have been, and still are great. To rise above, and shine, despite these challenges, is indeed a great feat.

I am so humbled by your tenth Shaykhah. Young, quiet, wife, mum. A silent unassuming giant of the Quraan in our midst. May Allaah preserve them all.

**MU'ALLIMAH KHADIJA ALLIE**

Executive member MJC, HOD of MJC Women's Forum

## *Reflective Questions*

After reading 10 Amazing Sheikhahs, here are some reflective questions to contemplate on and inspire you to take steps in working on your relationship with the Qur᾿ān:

1. What is your relationship with the Qur᾿ān like?

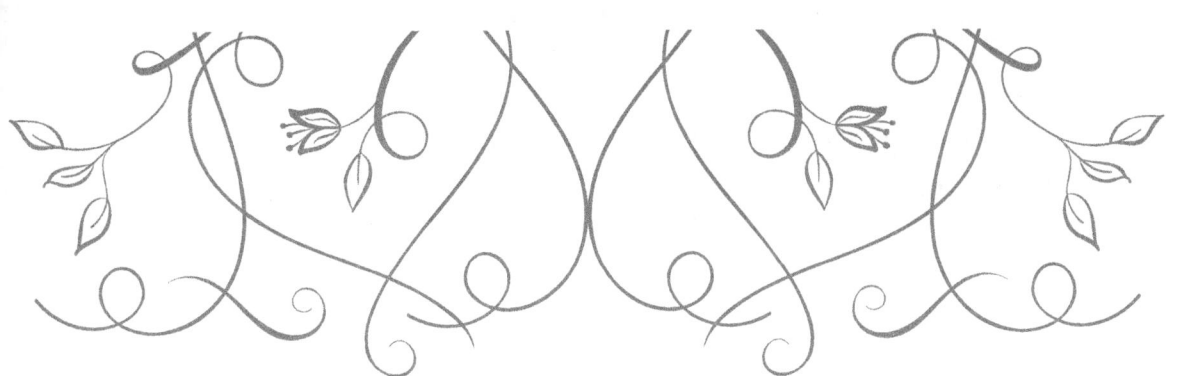

2. Has anything that you read in this booklet impacted your relationship with the Qurʾān?

3. Which Sheikhah or story inspired you the most?

4. How does this Sheikhah or story resonate with your own personal challenges and obstacles on your journey with the Qurʾān?

5. Which area in studying the Qurʾān would you like to improve on?

6. Which steps do you need to take to reach this goal?

# Bibliography


- *Imtāʿ al-Fuḍalāʾ bi Tarājim al-Qurrāʾ*: Ilyās ibn Aḥmad al-Barmāwī, Maktabah Dār al-Zamān, Medina, Kingdom of Saudi Arabia, 2nd Print, 2007.
- *Muʿjam al-Maʿājim wa al-Mashīkhāt*: Yūsuf ʿAbd al-Raḥmān al-Marʿashlī, Maktabat al-Rush, Riyadh, Kingdom of Saudi Arabia, 1st Print, 2002.
- *Al-Yāniʿ al-Janī min Asānid al-Shaykh ʿAbd al-Ghanī*: Muḥammad Muḥsin al-Tirhutī, Arwiqah li al-Dirāsāt wa al-Nashr, Amman, Jordon, 1st Print, 2016.
- *Pages From Cape Muslim History*: Yusuf da Costa & Achmat Davids, Naqshabandi-Muhammadi South Africa, Cape Town, South Africa, 2nd Impression, 2005.
- *Tashnīf al-Asmāʿ bi Shuyūkh al-Ijāzah wa al-Samāʿ*: Maḥmūd Saʿīd Mamdūḥ, Dār al-Kutub al-Miṣriyyah, Egypt, 2nd Print, 2013.

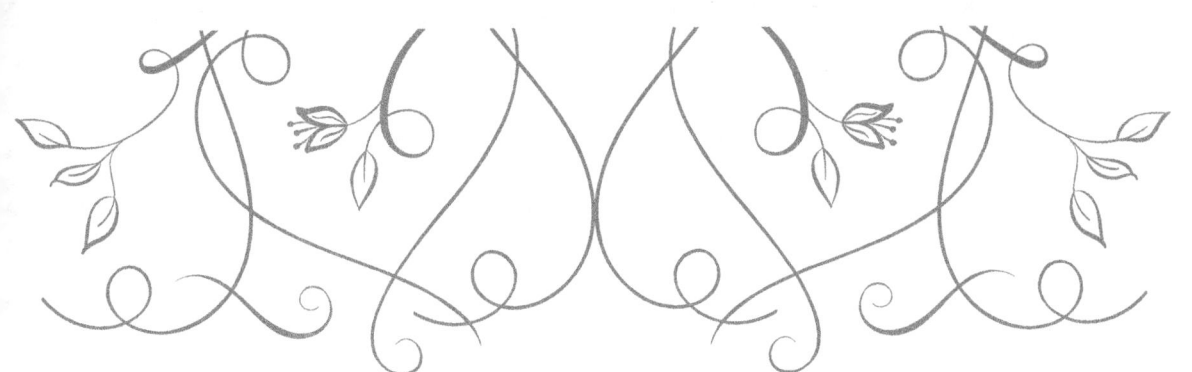

*Notes*

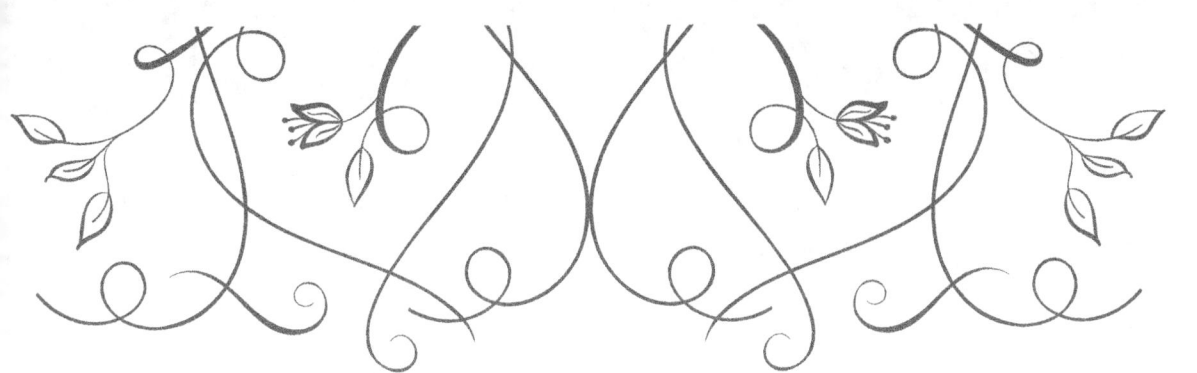

*Notes*

*Notes*

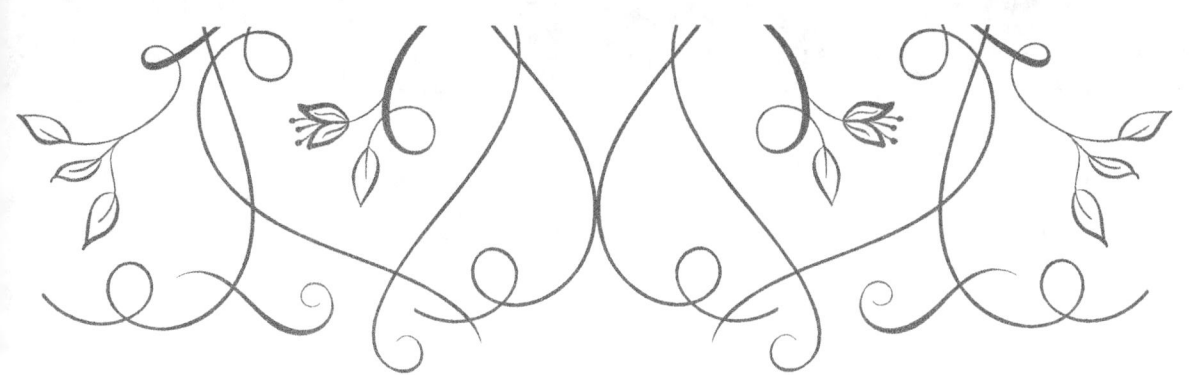

# *Notes*

*Notes*

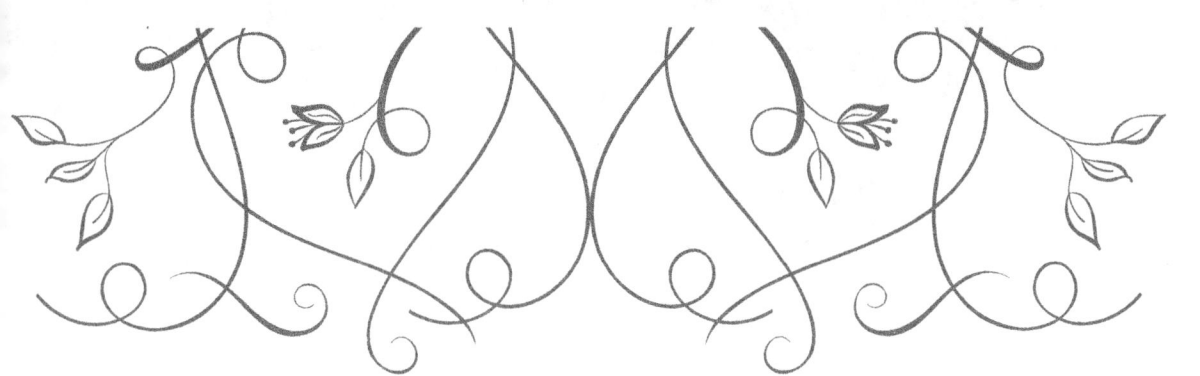

*Notes*

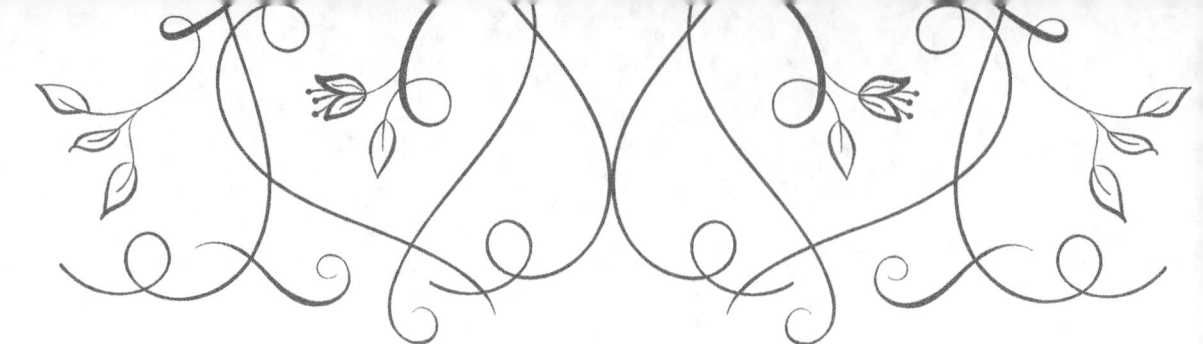

*Notes*

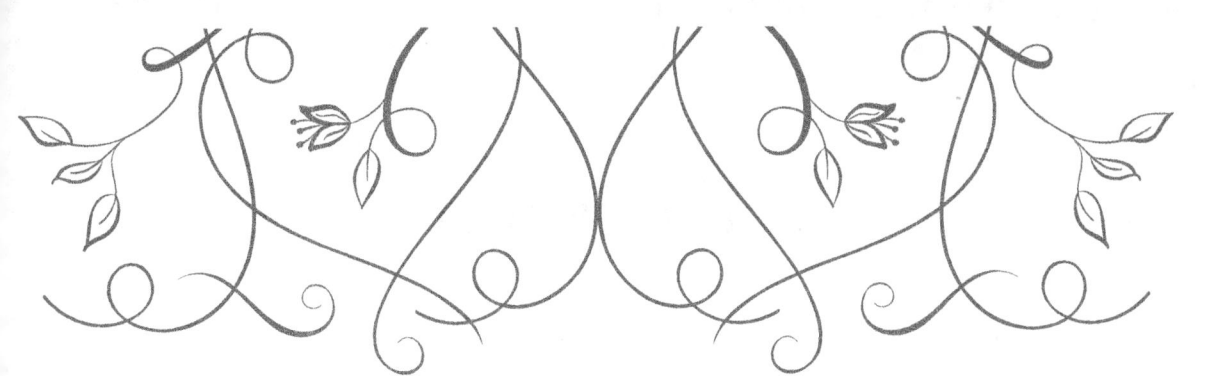

# OUR PUBLICATIONS



## Blessed Life of the Prophet Muhammad ﷺ

**Seeratul Mustafa ﷺ (Abridged): English Translation**

**Muhammad ﷺ - A Mercy unto mankind**

**Final Days of Rasulullah ﷺ**

**The Blessed Sunnah of Rasulullah ﷺ - Volumes 1, 2, 3**
*According to the Hanafi Mazhab*

**The Blessed Sunnah of Rasulullah ﷺ - Volume 1**
*According to the Shaafi'ee Mazhab*

**The Gift of Durood and Salaam**
*Virtues of Durood and Incidents regarding Love for Rasulullah ﷺ*

**Hajjatul Wadaa**
*The Farewell Hajj of Rasulullah* صلى الله عليه وسلم

**The Practice of Eighty Durood After Asr on Friday**

**The Selected Forty (Pocket Size)**
*Collection from Dalāil ul Khairāt*

## Women and Family

**Glimpses of True Beauty from the Lives of Pious Women (Vol. 1)**

**Glimpses of True Beauty from the Lives of Pious Women (Vol. 2)**

**Nurturing of Children (Parts 1 to 14)**

**Happily Ever After**
*A Muslimah's Guide to a Blissful Marriage*

**Tuhfatul Banaat**
*An ideal gift for the young daughters of the Ummah*

**Tuhfatush Shabaab**
*A gift for the Youth*

**Hijaab - In the light of the Qur'aan and Sunnah**

## Beliefs and Practices

**Al-Hizbul A'zam (Pocket Size)**

**Daily Wazaaif (Pocket Size)**
*Arabic* with *English*

**Masnoon Duas (Pocket Size)**
*Arabic* with *English*

**Islamic Manners**
*Shaykh Abdul Fattah Abu Ghuddah*

**Etiquettes for Students**
آداب المتعلمين

**Etiquettes for Teachers**
آداب المعلمين

**Fazail e Amaal (English)**
*Virtues of Actions*

**Fazail e Sadaqaat (English)**
*Virtues of Spending*

**Fazail e Ramadan (English)**
*Virtues of Ramadan*

**Fazail e Qurbaani (English)**
*Virtues of Sacrifice*

**Qurbaani in the Light of the Sunnah**

**Fasting In The Light Of The Sunnah**

**The Importance of Performing Salaah with Jamaat in the Musjid**

**The Adhan**

**Laws Regarding Trustees of Masaajid & Islamic Organisations**

## Lives of the Pious

**Rays of Radiance (Vol. 1)**
*Inspirational Incidents from the Lives of the Pious*

**Rays of Radiance (Vol. 2)**
*Inspirational Incidents from the Lives of the Pious*

**Scattered Pearls of Moulana Zakariyya Kandhelwi** رحمه الله

**Scattered Pearls of Moulana Ashraf Ali Thanwi** رحمه الله

**Scattered Pearls of Moulana Muhammad Ilyaas Kandhelwi** رحمه الله

**Hadhrat Mufti Mahmood Hasan Gangohi** رحمه الله

**Hadhrat Moulana Maseehullah Khan Saahib Sherwaani** رحمه الله

**The Life and Mission of Hadhrat Moulana Husain Ahmad Madani** رحمه الله

**Hadhrat Moulana Muhammad Qaasim Nanotwi** رحمه الله

# Arabic and Other Sciences

**From the Treasures of Arabic Morphology - من كنوز الصرف**

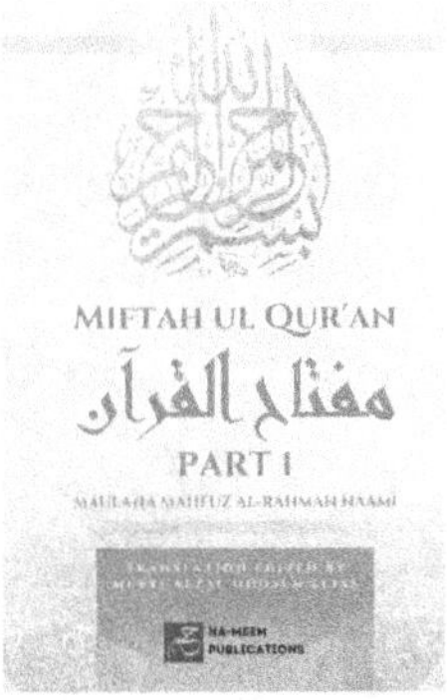


**Miftah ul Qur'an**
(Part 1, 2, 3, 4)

**The Ten Lessons of Arabic**

**The Cream of Arabic Imperative Words With Modern Words**

**Arabic Tutor: Arbi Ka Mu'allim**
(Volumes 1, 2, 3, 4)

**Solving Tarkeeb**
Translation of حَلّ تَرْكِيْب

**Qasas Un Nabiyyeen - Part 4**
*Arabic* with *English* Translation

**Sharh Miatu Amil**
شرح مائة عامل

# First Steps to Understanding

**First Steps to Understanding Sarf**

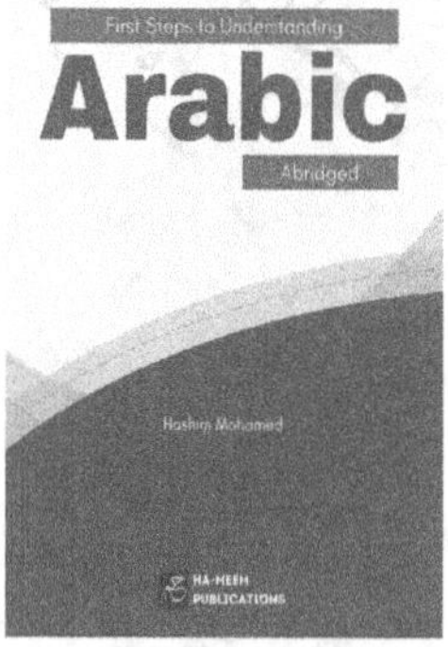


**First Steps to Understanding Arabic** ***(Abridged)***

**First Steps to Understanding Arabic**

**First Steps to Understanding Balagah**

**First Steps to Understanding Logic**

**First Steps to Understanding Urdu (2nd Edition)**

# Islamic Reflections and Worldview

**In Search of Mount Tur**

**Spiritual Light VS Material Might**

**Dhū al-Qarnayn and The Ya'jūj and Ma'jūj**

**Have You Pondered Over The Message Of Your Creator?**

**Understanding the Mahdi**

**How Should A Muslim View Modern Science?**

**In the Blessed Lands Jordan & Palestine**

**Spiritual Lessons Derived From SURAH AL-KAHF**

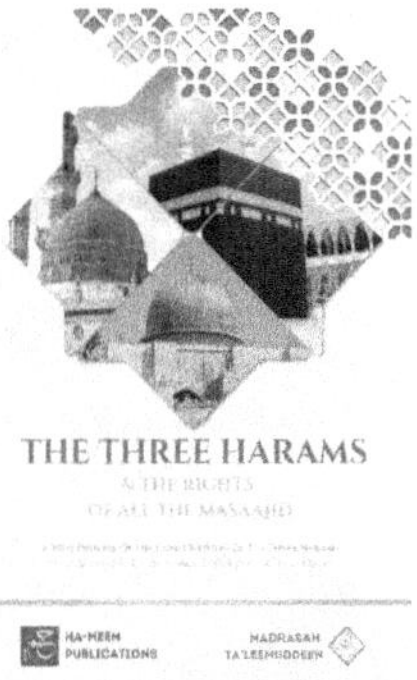


**The Three Harams**

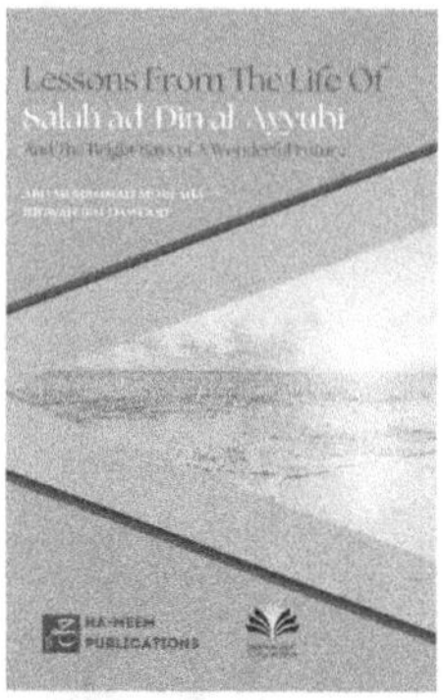


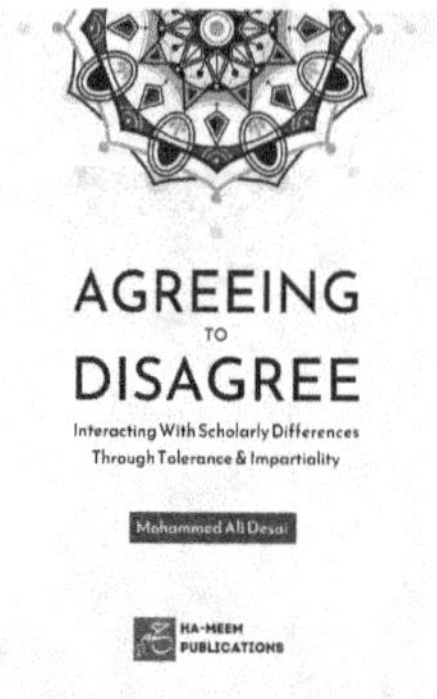


**Al-Aqsa - The Past, The Present, And The Future**

**Lessons From The Life Of Salah ad-Din al-Ayyubi**

**Agreeing To Disagree**

# Islamic Theology and Jurisprudence

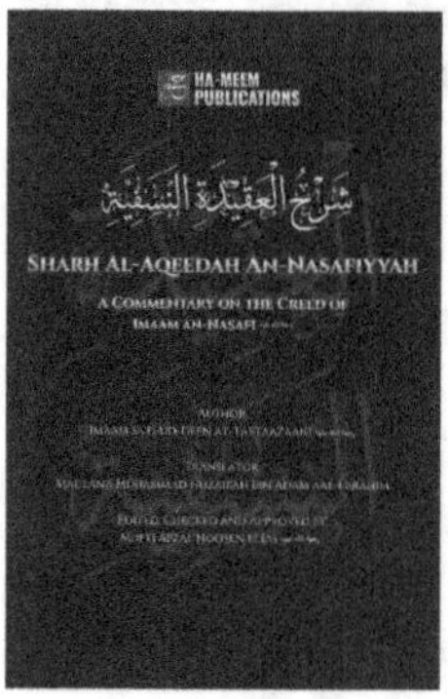


**Taleemul Haq**
Five Fundamentals of Islam

**Masail Al Qudoori Made Easy**
Question Answer Format (English)

**Sharh Al-Aqeedah An-Nasafiyyahs**
*English Translation*

**Simplified Principles of Fiqh**
Translation of آسان اصول فقه

**The Creed of Imam Tahawi**
*Arabic* with *English* & *Farsi* translation

## Specialized Texts in Qirā'āt

Fayd al-Mu'in (40 Hadith on the Virtues of the Qur'an)

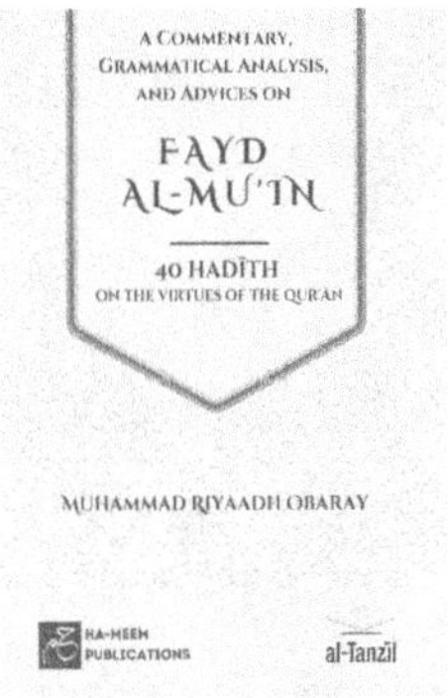


Commentary on Fayd al-Mu'in

Murshid al Qari - The Guide for Reciters of the Quran

A Commentary of the Tas-hil by Ihab Fikri

A Commentary of the Kāmil by Maḥmūd al-Sharqāwī

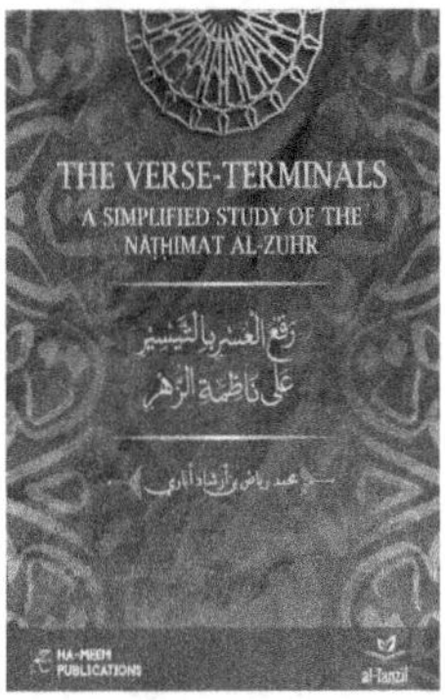


A Simplified Study of the Nāṭḥimat al-Zuhr

The Seven Variant Readings via the Shatibiyyah - Volume 1

The Gift to the Qurra

Nabr - Lexical Stress in the Quran

Nafaais al-Bayan

al-Tibyan - The Sequence of the Surahs

The Character of Ambassadors of The Quran

A Simplified Study of the Three Variant Readings via the Durrah

The Individual Variants of the Shatibiyyah and Durrah

40 Hadith on Qira'at

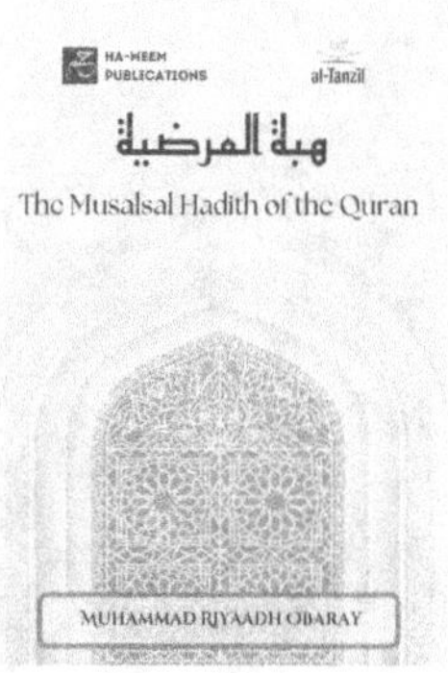


The Musalsal Hadith of the Quran

The Individual Variants of the Shatibiyyah

The Qurrā' of Desouk And Their Unique Transmission Chains

**Exposé of The Most Gracious, Most Kind on the Etiquette for Ambassadors of the Quran**

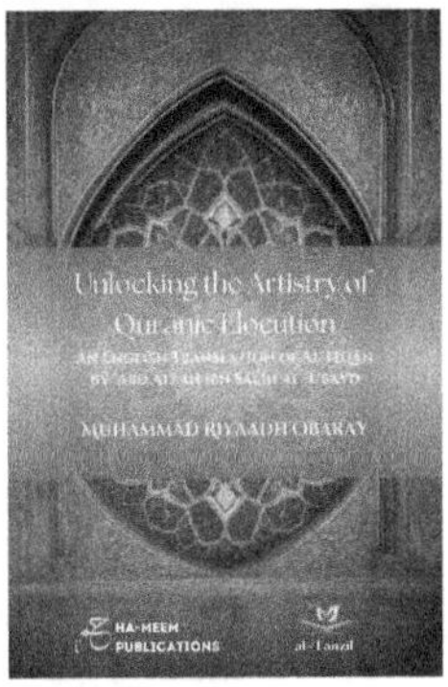


**Unlocking the Artistry of Quranic Elocution**

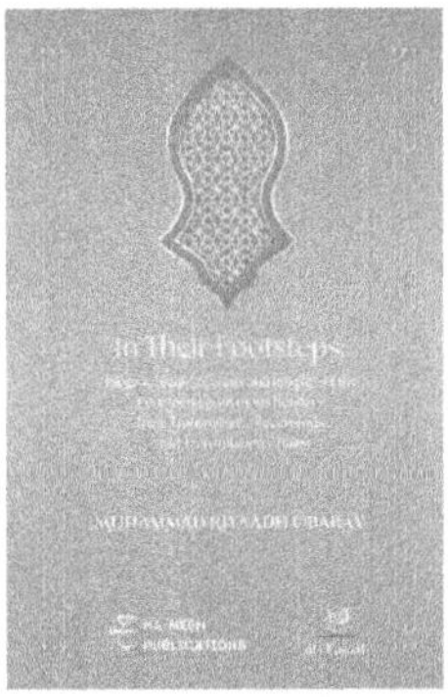


**In Their Footsteps - Biographical Accounts & Insights of the Fourteen Eponymous Readers**

**10 Amazing Sheikhahs**

**A Commentary of the Didactic Poem Al-Khāqāniyyah**

www.ingramcontent.com/pod-product-compliance
Lightning Source LLC
Chambersburg PA
CBHW080755120626
46557CB00006B/1282
* 9 7 8 1 9 9 8 6 6 9 0 1 1 *